My Wartime Wanderings

My Wartime Wanderings

*From the Western Desert to Berlin
With the 1st Battalion, the Rifle Brigade*

Kenneth L. Phillips

Edited by Ann Wiseman

THE CHOIR PRESS

First published in the United Kingdom in 2021 by
The Choir Press

ISBN 978-1-78963-174-6

The majority of photographs were taken by Ken using his own camera and film or where he appears in the photo by one of his army colleagues. Photographs from other sources are credited in the captions or were taken by family members. Maps have been produced specifically for this book. Place names have been left as written by Ken and are generally those in use by the army at the time.

Contents

❦

Introduction & Acknowledgements

My father Kenneth (Ken) Phillips didn't speak a lot to my sister or myself about his own experiences of the Second World War. He was, however, always interested in anything to do with the War and owned an extensive collection of books on the subject. When he retired in 1983 he typed up his memoirs, based largely on his diaries but also on letters which he had sent regularly during the war to his parents in England (these were typed up later by my grandmother). Dad sent his wartime diaries, the typed letter extracts and the wartime section of his memoirs to the Imperial War Museum in London.

On reading my copy of the memoirs again a few years ago I decided they were so interesting that they were deserving of a wider audience. This meant re-typing the memoirs to digitise them. My sister Chris read through all the letter extracts and typed out the most interesting and relevant of these. They are included in italics in the wartime section of this book at places where I hope they will enhance the text in some way.

For the purposes of this book I have summarised Dad's early years and post-war years, based on his original typewritten memoirs.

Huge thanks go to my husband, Ian, for all his work in checking through the text with me and also his valuable suggestions and additional research. Thanks also go to Chris for reading through the text and providing a great deal of help and very useful suggestions, as well as reading through and typing the letter extracts.

Thank you also to the Choir Press for their help and support in publishing the book, which I hope will make interesting and enjoyable reading.

Ann Wiseman

The Pre- War Years

A synopsis of my father's own written memoirs
about his life prior to the Second World War

Early Days
and Family Background

My father, Kenneth Laurence Phillips, was born on 13 August 1921 at 24 Braemar Avenue, Thornton Heath in South London. His father's family had a strong nautical background and came from Rotherhithe. His father, also called Kenneth, worked for Elders & Fyffes (the Fyffes Line) who at that time were the major importers of bananas into the country, mainly from the West Indies and Central America. Every week he brought home two hands of bananas which were ripened in the airing cupboard, so Ken junior (known as Laurie to his family) was well stuffed with bananas in his youth. His nickname throughout his childhood was 'Oxo', apparently the result of a popular advertisement of the time – 'Oxo builds bouncing babies'. He had an older sister, Joan, who was born in 1916.

Ken's maternal grandfather was a leather currier who set up his own business with a partner in Orange Walk in Bermondsey. When he retired the business was run by two of his sons. Ken's mother, Grace, also worked there for a few years doing the books and correspondence.

The family moved to a house in a new estate in Malden in Surrey in November 1925. They had electric light instead of gas and there were no power points, but they had no electric gadgets anyway. Malden at that time was still on the fringe of the countryside and they had to walk through fields of cows when they left the house until the Kingston bypass was built.

Ken went to school in September 1926 at Perth House, a small local school with two classrooms. In 1930, when he was just nine, Ken went to Tiffin School in Kingston. He started in a preparatory form called the Juniors and when he went into the first form proper he was only ten years and one month, compared with an average age of eleven years and three months. He felt that this affected his whole school career. Apart from having a struggle with the academic work he was a year behind in physical development when it came to sports, and tended to be put down by his classmates by words such as 'small boys should be seen and not heard'.

Ken took the General Schools/Matric Exam in June 1936 and as a result of a late sprint succeeded in getting his Matric (only ten out of 30 in the class managed to get their Matric). He used to go to school by train (even from the age of nine) and came home for lunch – only those who lived too far away had school dinners in those days. The cost amounted to just over a halfpenny per journey.

Ken enjoyed playing sport at school. There was PT (an hour twice a week) and on Wednesday afternoons they had rugger in the autumn and spring terms and cricket in the summer. They also had cross-country running in winter around Home Park and athletics in summer leading up to sports day. He always enjoyed these sports even though he felt he didn't shine. In rugby he started as a scrum half but reverted to the pack, which proved more rewarding. In his last year he was selected for the school 2nd XV, having worked his way up from the 4th and 3rd teams the previous year. He enjoyed going by coach to away games and remembered being rowed out to *HMS Worcester*, the old training ship moored off Greenwich, for tea after one game. In his last term he also played several games for the Old Boys.

Outside school Ken's time was fully occupied. Over the years his collection of Hornby trains, Meccano and model soldiers gradually increased, and great was his joy when the garage was fitted out with staging so that he could have a permanent layout without the chore of getting them out and putting them away every time. 'Pack them away, I want to lay the table' was the source of much bad temper. Collecting engine numbers was another pastime. Later he took to assembling Skybird model aeroplanes (not very well, he claimed).

'Going to the pictures' was a regular activity for most people – once a week was normal and many went twice. There were two cinemas in

Malden, one in Worcester Park and at least five in Kingston, as well as those in Wimbledon and Raynes Park. At weekends during the summer the family spent a lot of time at Elders & Fyffes sports ground, half an hour's walk from home. As Ken grew up he used to watch the cricket and often acted as scorer – a profitable activity as he got a shilling a game (a penny per head and two pennies from the skipper) as well as a free tea. His father used to play bowls and occasionally tennis and his sister Joan played tennis regularly. In the early days his father played hockey and later Ken sometimes used to go down with him to watch soccer.

From time to time during summer weekends the family went over to Hampton Court and walked along the Thames by Molesey Lock, watching the antics of the people on the river. There were also occasional visits to and from relatives and friends. Going to family in Streatham meant catching a train to Wimbledon, then one to Streatham (in the early days this was by steam train before the building of the Wimbledon-Sutton line and the onset of electrification), and then a bus up the Common. Less frequently there were visits to relatives in Bromley, which meant changing also at Herne Hill, always a long and draughty wait, but with a chance of unusual engine numbers.

The summer holiday was an eagerly awaited annual event, with weeks of anticipation. They were nearly all seaside holidays with a hut on the beach and the time spent swimming and playing on the sand. The family travelled down by train, with two trunks sent *passengers' luggage in advance* which were collected by horse and cart on the Thursday. These would be in the hotel bedroom waiting for them when they arrived on the Saturday.

After getting his Matric the question of a career loomed ahead, even though Ken was still under fifteen. He thought of going into the Navy, in the paymaster branch, but his father rejected this on the grounds (correct at that time) that one could not afford to be a naval officer without a private income. The Merchant Service was also rejected because many ships were laid up as the result of the slump and crews were ten a penny. A friend of Ken's had just got into the civil

Ken in the garden at New Malden - Sept 1937

service and gone to the Air Ministry and it struck Ken that if he did the same he might be able to get into the Admiralty. He therefore decided to sit for the civil service exam – clerical grade. (At that time it was highly regarded and there was great competition to get in.)

The problem was that he was now just fifteen and could not sit the exam, the syllabus for which was comparable to the general schools, until he was sixteen. This meant waiting eighteen months until January 1938. He was therefore allowed to stay on at school to do his own work. There were plenty of other distractions so he had a very enjoyable time but did not exert a great deal of effort. He eventually sat the exam but failed. This news came on 22 April and agitated his father, who started scanning the situations vacant in the *Daily Telegraph*. He found the Eagle Star Insurance Company wanted a smart lad and Ken was told to apply for that. He was accepted and started work at 32, Moorgate on 16 May 1938 at a salary of £60 a year.

The office work itself was mainly straightforward arithmetic, for which he had the benefit of a calculating machine and sets of tables with which to prepare quotations for companies thinking of starting pension schemes. He enjoyed his first full rugger season playing for various teams at Old Tiffinians RFC. By now the war clouds were gathering. He went down to *HMS President* to try to enrol as a writer but they were full up. He therefore turned his attention to the army and approached the London Rifle Brigade, who were full but put Ken on their waiting list. At the end of March 1939 the government suddenly decided to double the size of the Territorial Army overnight, so on 4 April 1939 Ken swore his oath and became part of the Second Battalion, the London Rifle Brigade. Being just over seventeen and a half, Ken escaped the indignity of having the rank of 'boy', instead of 'rifleman', which was the fate of those under that age.

The next five months were fairly hectic. They had drills on two nights a week, followed by ham rolls and beer or shandy in tankards in the 'Green Room'. Ken managed to get away for a fortnight's sailing holiday on the Norfolk Broads with a couple of friends in early June. They thoroughly enjoyed the break although they were all in-experienced sailors.

Soon after coming back from holiday Ken was given an unusual job. The risk of war was now such that companies were starting to make preparations and Eagle Star had bought Cobham Hall in Surrey to use if it was necessary to evacuate the London office. They decided to move all their policies and similar documents down there, and Ken spent ten days at Cobham unloading the vanloads of policies as they arrived, stacking them on racks in the right order. He broke off to go to the TA camp at Burley, near Ringwood, in the New Forest for the last week in July and first in August. By then they had their uniforms, equipment and rifles, and could move about in formation in good order, but route marches in new boots were somewhat painful. They were kept busy on various exercises chasing round the countryside, but unfortunately it proved to be a very wet fortnight; it rained as they were marched up to camp from Holmsley Station by the LRB buglers, and it rained when they were piped down again by the pipers of the London Scottish at the end of camp. The night before they left they had to spend in hastily arranged billets in Brockenhurst as their tents were awash, but as it turned out it was all useful experience.

After a couple of weeks back at the office, during which Ken reached his eighteenth birthday, he was sent down to Cobham again on Thursday, 24 August, on which day he also received the first warning notice: 'Be prepared to report to this headquarters immediately.' He worked at Cobham all through the weekend, but on Monday morning, the 28th, he got his final notice: 'You are hereby called out for military service from 28 August under Section 1 of the Reserve and Auxiliary Forces Act, 1939.' Discarding his civvies for the duration, Ken donned his uniform and caught his morning train up to town for the last time, called in at the office to say goodbye, and then reported to Bunhill Row.

My Wartime Wanderings

⟨⟩

*In the Western Desert, Italy and Northwest Europe
With 5 Platoon, B Company, 1st Battalion,
the Rifle Brigade*

K L Phillips 6969044
Rifleman, Lance Corporal, Corporal and Sergeant

With the London Rifle Brigade

❧

I joined the 2nd Battalion, the London Rifle Brigade at 130 Bunhill Row, in the City of London, on 4 April 1939. I had been on their waiting list since the previous autumn and the opportunity came when the government suddenly announced their decision to double the strength of the Territorial Army overnight. It was regarded as one of the 'crack' TA units and was the second in the country (after the London Scottish) to complete both battalions to full strength (632 men in each). We used to go for drills two nights a week, fired our 'classification' on the ranges at Bisley at Whitsun, and spent a fortnight in camp near Ringwood in the New Forest in the last week in July and first in August. On 24 August I had the first warning telegram: 'Be prepared to report to this headquarters immediately', followed by several detailing what I should bring with me, including 24 hours of rations. The final one came on 28 August, a fortnight after my eighteenth birthday: 'You are hereby called out for military service from 28 August under Sec. 1 of the Reserve and Auxiliary Forces Act, 1939'.

When I arrived at Bunhill Row I found that only our platoon and a few key men had been called up, possibly for some special job that did not materialise, because we did nothing for a couple of days except sandbag filling. On 1 September the main body of the battalion was called up, and we helped with the embodiment procedure, in which all the pages in everyone's AB3 had to be filled in and sent off to various destinations. If I remember right I was in charge of a stamp marked 'Fit A1' which I stamped on the appropriate page. There was not room for everyone in the drill hall, even though the 1st Battalion had moved to Wellington Barracks, and my company ('F') moved into the gym in the basement of the City of London College in Ropemaker Street close by. It was fine except when some of the lads came back from the pub in the evenings and were tempted to display their prowess on the wall-bars, ropes and vaulting horses, to the mortal danger of all around. On the Sunday morning when war was declared I was on guard outside the front door armed with a walking-out cane, when the air raid siren sounded half an hour later. I marched smartly inside to the company commander and reported this and was told to shut the grill across the door and stand behind it. This was apparently to stop panic-stricken civilians from rushing in and endeavouring to shelter with the troops!

We spent the next month there. It was very much a '1914-18' army in those days. Our rifles and equipment had in fact been in store since then, although we now marched in threes instead of fours, had battledress instead of service dress and side-caps which were designed to fall off with every sudden motion, such as arms drill. We had only two trucks in the battalion, and two Bren guns with which each company could practice on one day a week. So apart from sandbagging, we did some arms drill, PT and had several marches through the City to encourage the population. Several times we went to Rainham ranges to fire rifle and Bren, and apart from guarding our billet I had one guard on Tower Bridge. Our guardroom was at the top of one of the bascules, 89 steps up and no room to pass if one met someone halfway in full kit. We had our uniforms but no greatcoats at that time and as it was starting to get chilly we were given civilian overcoats. Great care was taken to try to ensure the sentries on guard at the same time had similar coats on; the platoon sergeant appropriated a very smart 'Teddy Bear' coat for himself.

On 8 October (we always seemed to move on Sundays) we made the first of the ten moves we were to make in the next ten months to Northwood to guard the headquarters of the RAF Coastal Command. Here we lived in Nissen huts and messed with the RAF (run by NAAFI), and spent nearly all our time on guard – about four nights in a row followed by a day when we could go home, unless we were on a day guard or there was something else on. Most of the night guards were 'prowler guards' where we roamed around the place with pick-helves, but there was one ceremonial guard on the front gate which continued during the day as well. For one week at the end of October, and again at the end of November, one section was detached to guard a railway bridge near Ruislip. We lived in a bell tent pitched beside the line and, as the weather was getting a bit cold and wet, we tried to keep a coal fire going in a brazier thanks to the engine drivers, who would throw out a couple of knobs of coal as they steamed past. If we were running a bit low we would shout out 'coal', but one driver must have been new on the job because he banged his arms across his chest and replied 'Yes it is, isn't it.' One or two passengers used to throw us their evening papers too. At the end of our second spell there we moved to Northolt aerodrome, guarding the Hurricanes of 111 and Blenheims of 604 Squadrons. The Blenheims had just been on a raid to, I think, Wilhelmshaven, which had not gone too well, and the station commander was livid because he said the operation was being talked about in all the pubs in Ruislip the night before they went. While here we were billeted in an infants' school; we slept on the floor and the tables and chairs did not matter, but the lavatories were a bit of a problem.

On 12 December we moved to Beckenham, to old Victorian houses which were empty in Copers Cope Road and The Avenue. Battalion HQ and the cookhouse were in two of the bank sports grounds at the far end from us, near New Beckenham station (we were at the Beckenham Junction end) so we had a very long walk for meals. The weather got really cold and, as the houses were unfurnished, there was no heating and the pipes froze so we had no water. Arrangements were made for the people in the road to accept two squaddies each to wash and shave at their house in the mornings; most of us also got a cup of tea and the really lucky ones were also given breakfast, saving themselves from a long walk there and back to the cookhouse. I had a week's leave soon after arriving and I was able to get home again on Christmas Day after church parade and also to visit my grandparents in Streatham on Boxing Day. On New Year's Eve we spent twelve hours in the Railway Hotel at Beckenham Junction. We went in at noon and when the bar closed repaired to the lounge where we waited until we could get tea and toast. The bar opened again at six and we saw the New Year in at midnight; it was much warmer than the billet. We stayed at Beckenham for the first six weeks of the year, with drill, route marches, weapon training and some field exercises in Beckenham Place Park. There were also occasional fatigues; peeling sacks of potatoes with cold water out in the open with snow on the ground is not to be recommended. We went to Croydon Aerodrome on two or three occasions, taking up positions to defend the airfield, which was our emergency task.

On 10 February we moved to the Millwall Docks, guarding the graving dock, the boiler house, wharves etc. for a month. Our quarters were in a loft over an office belonging to Green and Silley Weir, the ship repairers. There was a procession of ships coming into the dry dock to have degaussing cables fitted as a protection against magnetic mines – the *Gloucester Castle*, *Agra Marina*, *Jamaica Pioneer*, *Markhor* and *City of Karachi*. A much sought-after post was at one of the entrance gates where some road works were going on and there was a night watchman who had a brazier round which we could sit during the small hours. The fumes tended to make one sleepy but we had an arrangement with the docks police, who had phones in their huts. As soon as the orderly officer walked in one gate, the police there rang round all the other gates to warn the sentries.

On 11 March we moved to the Abbey Road Building Society sports ground at Kenton, Middlesex, where we got down to training again: drill, weapon training, route marches, trench digging, bayonet fighting, field exercises and some night operations. Whilst there, the Germans invaded first Denmark and Norway and then France and Belgium. That was the day we moved once more, this time to the Elder Road Children's Home, South Norwood – a somewhat undignified address. There was a bit of a panic at first and we had to stand to, night and morning, in case of enemy paratroops, but it calmed down later. We spent a lot of time digging, but where and why I cannot recall. For the first time since the war started we were all together as a battalion so there was an increased amount of bull, with RSM's drill parades, battalion quarter guards and so on. We spent one day charging around Streatham Common and on another occasion practiced an emergency turnout to Banstead Downs, with Company HQ in the asylum, although what we were supposed to be defending I never knew. We also spent a week at Bisley on the ranges. Because of the invasion scare we had all been issued with live rounds, which we kept in our ammunition pouches. One day during weapon training some clot loaded his rifle with a clip of live ammunition. Luckily we heard the rasp of the rounds going into the magazine and yelled out – we were using aiming discs at the time and his first shot would have gone into someone's eye at five yards range.

On 16 June (a Sunday of course) we were on the move again by train to Wisbech on a route which entailed many stops. When these occurred where there were houses backing on to the line, people came rushing out with pots of tea, apparently under the impression that we'd just been evacuated from France – it didn't stop us from accepting the tea! We spent a week manning a roadblock at a village named Guyhirn where one of us fired the battalion's first shot in anger at a car which failed to stop at the block. It was strongly suspected to contain aircrew from one of the nearby RAF airfields, but I don't think anyone was hit. After only a week we moved again on the next Sunday up to Cannock Chase outside Rugeley, where we were under canvas with the rest of the brigade – the London Scottish and Queen's Westminsters. After a game of snooker in Rugeley and an ENSA concert with Ralph Reader we moved on again the following Sunday to Ingestre Hall, Great Haywood, outside Stafford. Here we stayed a full five weeks and actually got down to some training: weapons training, grenade throwing, route marches, trench digging, night ops, patrolling, advance guards, rearguards, etc. One of the most amusing was the drill for dealing with aircraft attack. Marching in columns of threes, on the command 'aircraft action' we had to come to a halt and stand there blazing away with our rifles, whereas as they had already learned in France the only sensible thing to do was to fling yourself into the nearest ditch. We used to march into Stafford for a bath and then get all hot and sticky marching back again. Off duty we got into the pictures in Stafford sometimes or visited the local pub, the Coach and Horses.

We moved off again, on a Monday this time but it was August bank holiday, to the Miner's Rest at Porthcawl in South Wales. I went straight into the sick bay with impetigo, possibly coming from dirty blankets which were unwashed and unchanged after nearly twelve months sleeping in tents and on dusty floors. After two days I was sent off to the Bridgend Emergency Hospital where I was stuck for five weeks with violet unction all over my face. It was a civilian hospital which had been cleared for possible air raid casualties. I never saw any of it except our own ward, which contained about eight, including a couple more from the LRB, two or three South Wales Borderers and a Dutch policeman who was very concerned as to the fate of his family. Life was very boring, enlivened only by one air raid warning when we spotted a German bomber that had sneaked in and dropped a couple of bombs on the RAF airfield at Stormy Down. Just after my birthday, however, I was shattered to see in the Saturday morning paper a photograph of bomb damage that I recognised as being by the station near my home. I think they were going for Croydon Aerodrome but had been intercepted and dropped their bombs on the railway line instead. Some of the shops near the station were hit and our newspaper man and greengrocer were both killed. My family helped clear up the mess when the house of friends living on the corner of our road was machine-gunned, whether on purpose or in the confusion of a dogfight I don't know. On the Monday morning I was very relieved to get a letter from home saying all was well. I finally left hospital on Friday 13 September and was very upset to be told to report to the 2nd Motor Training Battalion at Tidworth instead of going back to the LRB at Porthcawl. Disobeying orders on the excuse of having to collect my kit, I went back to Porthcawl but they wouldn't have anything to do with me. A War Office instruction had just been issued under which anyone who had been in hospital for over three weeks had to be struck off strength and posted back to the regimental holding battalion and they said I would no doubt soon be able to get back on a draft. So I set off next day very dismally on the cross-country train journey to Tidworth, eventually arriving at Lucknow Barracks late in the evening and spending the night in the guardroom.

Next morning I was posted to D Company, 2nd Motor Training Battalion which was the 'odds and sods' company with a floating population of people coming from various postings or hospital and disappearing from time to time in different directions. The other companies consisted of recruits in training. I saw the company commander who said he would do his best to see I got back to the LRB but, as it transpired, this amounted to nothing. The next three to four months were the most miserable I spent in the army. Leaving the chaps I had known for eighteen months, and lived with night and day for twelve months, I was now on my own and part of no cohesive group. Also, as Territorials and volunteers, when we were given a job to do we all mucked in and got it done, but the attitude of some of the conscripts was different, as we had found when some of them were first drafted to us at the beginning of 1940. Half a dozen of us might be on a fatigue when we would suddenly realise that two were missing, having skived off. Since the job had to be done this meant more work for those remaining, which was not the way we were used to things and resulted in closer supervision by NCOs. Moreover, although the LRB was affiliated to the Rifle Brigade, it was a different regiment with a different cap badge and I had no wish to change my allegiance. However, there was nothing I could do about it.

I was kept fairly active with plenty of fatigues; Officers' Mess, Sergeants' Mess, cookhouse, dining room, canteen, QM stores, road sweeping and coal, the latter being one of the favourites. It involved taking a truck to the railway siding and loading it up with coal, which we took round to the various offices, messes etc. and also to the married quarters. This gained us temporary favour with some of the sergeants in the hope that we would drop off an extra bucket at their house, whilst we also got the odd cup of tea from some of the wives for the same reason. Also we were able to slip a bucket or two into our own hut as the ration was not nearly enough to keep the fire going. Otherwise we used to creep down to the siding in dead of night to pinch a bucket-full from there. We also had a lookout post on nearby Clarendon Hill, where I periodically spent a night searching the sky for German paratroops, or a day on AA picquet, ready to shoot down with a Bren any German plane which might have the temerity to attempt to drop a bomb on Tidworth. Luckily we escaped the ceremonial of battalion quarter guard as this was left to the recruits. Any spare time was taken up with a spot of drill or weapon training and we also had one twenty-mile cycle ride. In those days the army's method of dealing with German tanks was to have a platoon of cyclists who were supposed to ride up to them with Molotov cocktails (petrol bombs). As I had hardly ever ridden a bike and army bicycles were built on motorcycle lines I was more than saddle-sore at the end of it. In the evenings there were two cinemas, the Hippodrome and a fleapit called the Electric, and also the garrison theatre which had live shows. I hardly used the NAAFI as there were a couple of other canteens which were much better. I think one was the C of E and the other the RC. I also had about half a dozen games of rugger playing for the battalion against other units at Tidworth.

During this time the Blitz on London was at its height and my father arranged for my mother and sister to get away to Exmouth to stay with friends for a time. I managed to get up to London to see him one Saturday, and a fortnight later at the end of November I had seven days leave which I spent at Exmouth. This was just after I was appointed 'permanent company runner' which meant sitting in the office all day, running errands and keeping the fire going; a cushy job but hardly enthralling. Soon after coming back from leave I found that they were sending a draft back to the LRB, but when I tried to get on it they said I could not go because I was not 'motor trained'. The LRB were converting to a motor battalion and everyone going there had to be so trained. I pointed out that none of the LRB were motor trained anyway but this cut no ice, so I asked to be motor trained myself so I could get back to them on a later draft. This they agreed to and I was immediately transferred to the motor training company. Driving instruction started with a 15-cwt truck in a field and progressed to a Humber car on the road. We usually went to Marlborough or

Salisbury, spent too long in the canteen and then had to belt back to barracks. Most of the others in my batch had done a bit of driving before so they got most of it, and ten or fifteen minutes driving at a time did not give me the chance to get the hang of it. Christmas was quiet – my diary says 'reading and writing letters' with a variety show at the garrison theatre in the evening, whilst Boxing Day was spent reading all day and a film called 'House of Seven Gables' in the evening.

Soon afterwards, on 3 January, I found my name down for a draft to the 1st Bn, the Rifle Brigade. I immediately protested that I was LRB, not RB, but got nowhere. I then said that I could not go because I was not yet motor trained. The clerk said 'Let's have your AB64', stamped 'motor trained' in it and gave it back. I then sought an interview with the welfare officer who was himself a Territorial (1914/18 vintage) from the Artists Rifles, but all I got was a homily on what an honour it was for a Territorial to be allowed to serve in a regular battalion. I thought this was a bit rich in view of the fact that the regular battalion had been put in the bag at Calais, and was now comprised, almost entirely, of conscripts. So with a sad heart I changed my 'Primus in Urbe' cap badge for a 'Prince Consort's Own' and took myself and my kit across the road to Jellalabad Barracks where the 1st Bn had been training since they had reformed after Calais. Of course I settled down there eventually and saw a lot more of the world than I would if I had remained with the LRB, who stayed in England, a lot of the time in Yorkshire, until they followed us to Normandy in July 1944, nearly three years after I had gone overseas. They must have been bored to death in that time.

With 1st Battalion, the Rifle Brigade in England

❧⟡❧

The battalion were in the process of moving to Farnham and most of them had already gone. I followed next morning and was posted to B Company, 5 Platoon, who were billeted at Goldhill Manor, Lower Bourne, south of Farnham on the Hindhead road. 5 Platoon was the scout platoon, equipped with tracked carriers, each with a crew of three. We had eleven of these, together with a couple of Dingos (scout cars) and some despatch riders. I was glad of this as it was a much more interesting job than in the three motor platoons in the company. Each of those had three sections of eight men who went round in a 15-cwt truck but had to get out on their flat feet when they went into action, whereas we stayed mobile. There were 42 of us in the platoon when we went abroad; two of us were still with it when the war ended. The platoon commander was Tommy Redfern, a big chap who played cricket for Richmond and rugger for Rosslyn Park. He was later killed by a Hurricane in the desert in June 1942.

We were at Farnham for five months and kept very busy, training in the carriers on Frensham Common, Thursley Common, Hankley Common and the country round about. There were brigade and divisional schemes lasting two or three days reaching as far as Petersfield, Arundel, Chichester and Tenterden. Maintaining and cleaning the carriers took up a good deal of time. We all had to practice driving carriers, Dingos and motorcycles. I didn't mind the carriers but never enjoyed the motorcycles. The Dingo scared me stiff in reverse; it had the same gears in reverse as forwards and four-wheel steering. Doing 40 mph backwards trying to crane one's neck to look out through a slit at the winding road ahead was no joke. We practiced activities like river crossings and roadblocks as well as the usual weapon training and drill parades, fifteen-mile route marches and firing on the ranges at Borden and Longmoor. The schemes involved a lot of convoy driving. We travelled with gaps of 50 yards between vehicles and 150 yards between groups as a precaution against air attack (and to let other traffic in) and with all our vehicles the company occupied just over a mile of road and the battalion about six miles. If the whole brigade was on the road it covered some 25 to 30 miles. The usual speed was fifteen miles 'in the hour', which included a twenty minute stop every two hours, but invariably while the leading vehicle was crawling along at a steady twenty mph those at the back were doing over 40, not easy in a carrier, trying desperately to keep up. Often a night drive was involved, usually on the way home when people were tired anyway. This was not easy with no lights except a dim one under the rear axle of each vehicle and no street lights or signposts. I distinguished myself on one occasion by leading the whole battalion up a track into a farmyard, turning round and coming out again (which meant passing every vehicle in the column as I did so). Trying to read my map with a torch in a jolting carrier, I had turned off about half a mile too soon. When I got my ticking off afterwards, my comment – that if every other vehicle commander had been doing his own map reading as he should then no one would have followed me – was coldly received. The carriers invariably led when the battalion was on the move as they had some degree of armour and were more manoeuvrable in action. The platoon commander travelled behind the leading section and the leading section commander was in the middle of his three carriers. The leading vehicle was therefore probably commanded by a lance corporal. Since the leading vehicle would almost inevitably be knocked out on reaching an enemy roadblock, it was considered that the loss of a lance corporal could more easily be borne than that of a subaltern or sergeant. Similarly, when working with the tanks, a carrier section usually went ahead of the tanks, because it was cheaper to replace a carrier than a tank.

From time to time we had to do a guard, either MT Picqet (guarding the vehicles) or battalion quarter guard. Luckily the companies were too widely dispersed around Farnham for battalion drill parades, so the RSM's only opportunity to get at the troops was when they were on quarter guard. Like most RSMs, ours was a great character whose bark was worse than his bite. On one occasion he walked along the rank looking at everyone's cap and saying 'dirty cap badge' until he came to one chap whose cap badge was his pride and joy; it was really gleaming. The RSM looked at his cap and said 'dirty ...' stopped, looked down, said 'dirty boots' and passed on to the next man with a 'dirty cap badge'. After the guard-mounting he took us in hand to demonstrate the sentry's challenge; 'Halt, who goes there?' followed by 'Advance friend and be recognised' and then 'Pass, friend, all's well.' He made each of us bellow it out in turn, then pointed to a window just above and said, 'I sleep up there and I want to hear every challenge the sentry makes during the night.' I was on guard later and from about 11 pm onwards the chaps from Battalion HQ were returning in dribs and drabs from an evening in Farnham. I duly challenged each one until suddenly the window above was opened with a crash and the RSM shouted, 'Sentry, how can I get to sleep when you keep making that bloody noise?'

Farnham was very handy for the evenings and weekends. There were two cinemas, the Regal and the County, and a number of canteens or else we went for a drink in the Cricketers. In February I had a week's leave with every night being punctuated by air raid warnings.

At the end of March I was appointed temporary unpaid lance corporal and didn't enjoy it very much. It is, I think, the worst rank in the army. One is at everybody's beck and call, having to pass on most of the orders to the troops but having the least authority. Before a week was out I was in trouble, having been seen coming out of the cinema with a rifleman. One lived, ate and slept with them but wasn't supposed to spend spare time with them, but I had no intention of dropping my friends. I got on well with the platoon commander and platoon sergeant but not with the company commander and CSM who used to chase me regularly. I could do the practical part of my job without trouble but was not a good 'barrack square' NCO.

My next leave, at the end of May, came just as the battalion moved to Swindon, where our platoon was billeted in an empty house on the Bath Road – No. 25, I think. We had one exercise on Salisbury Plain to Blandford then they came round seeking volunteers for a draft to the Middle East, failing which people would be detailed. Being a bit browned off with things as they were and bearing in mind that many of my colleagues were married, I volunteered, went off to 2nd MTB next day, and was home on a week's embarkation leave the next day.

The day after I returned to Tidworth I found myself back with the battalion at Swindon. Whilst I was on leave they had realised that I was not yet twenty and therefore too young to be allowed overseas. They changed the regulation later in the war and we had eighteen-year-olds in Normandy. We went straight off to the plain on another scheme and then moved to Windmill Hill, Tidworth under canvas for four weeks. These were mostly spent on divisional exercises on Salisbury Plain, one of which was watched by the King, Queen and princesses, after which we had to drive up and line the road as they walked past. I got a bit concerned when Princess Elizabeth left her party and started looking into the vehicles lined up behind us, because I had left a half-eaten cheese sandwich about two inches thick in the front of my carrier, but luckily she returned to the road before reaching it. We drew our own conclusions from this visit and were proved right when they told us on 9th August that we were going overseas. We returned to Swindon on the 11th, went on embarkation leave on the 12th and I had my twentieth birthday on the 13th. After we got back we spent the next month checking all our vehicles and equipment, drawing tropical kit and doing a certain amount of training. Periodically we used to march down to the public baths at the bottom of the hill, have a bath and march smartly back up the hill again. Being in town, it was easy to get to a cinema (the Arcadia, Savoy or Regal) and there were visits to canteens, a milk bar round the corner and, more frequently, the Cross Keys. In the meantime I had given up my stripe. Neither I nor the company commander were happy with it and in any case the vacancy had been filled whilst I was on embarkation leave for the first time, so I happily returned to the

In the garden at New Malden. Embarcation leave, August 1941.

Ken with his mother

Ken with his father

Ken with his sister Joan

ranks. I was able to slip away for the day twice and get home before we boarded the train on 24 September and, travelling via Oxford, Leicester and Berwick, arrived in Glasgow next morning. At midday we boarded the *RMS Strathaird*, our home for the next nine weeks, whilst our vehicles went on the *Clan Campbell*.

En Route to North Africa

❦

Strathaird was a P&O liner of 22,284 GRT (Gross Registered Tonnage) which used to be on the run to the Far East and Australia. She survived the war and was scrapped in 1961. I don't know how many troops there were on board but they included our battalion and the 9th Lancers, plus a lot of other drafts and details including some RAF and Royal Marines. The latter always affected an air of superiority when we were at sea. Our mess deck was a scene of chaos as soon as we reached it; it seemed impossible that so many people could fit into such a confined space. Previously, in billets, barracks or tents we each had our own bit of bed-space but here all we had was a few inches of shelf on which to store our kitbag and pack, etc. There were long mess tables and benches at which we sat to eat, write, read or play cards. At night we slept in hammocks or on the deck or mess tables. I was lucky enough to get a hammock, which was quite comfortable once one had learned how to control it, except when some misguided joker coming off guard at the crack of dawn would decide to slip the lashing. Landing feet first wasn't too bad, but head first could be painful. In the hammock one couldn't feel the ship rocking but if it was pitching and tossing it was less comfortable. We were on 'G' deck well below the waterline, and somewhere between the galley and engine room, so it was pretty warm and the standard dress was PT shorts and plimsolls. We were aboard for three days before we moved downstream to Greenock where the convoy was assembling, during which time we sorted ourselves and, of course, practiced boat stations. After we had duly assembled and been told what to do when the alarm bells sounded, someone asked, 'Which is our boat?' 'Oh, there isn't a boat,' was the answer, 'you just have to jump into the water when ordered to abandon ship.'

Two days later at dusk we moved off through the boom and off out to sea. There was a strip of deck on which we were allowed but it was a bit blowy in the North Atlantic and one had to keep on the move. On the second day out one of the destroyers dropped a few depth charges but there was no sign of a U-boat and the following morning a Focke-Wulf recce plane (shufti-kite as we came to call them in the desert) appeared on the horizon. We had to go below as soon as the alarm bells went, much to our disgust. It was suggested that this was to give the crew a free hand to get away if the ship sank! Some of our chaps were lucky enough to be on permanent AA picquet, manning Bren guns mounted in the dummy funnel, but I was condemned to periodic guards on watertight doors in the bowels of the ship and I eventually succumbed to seasickness when on guard on 'H' deck, right aft above the propellers. I was OK until some of the chaps around me rushed for the bucket and then I had to follow suit.

The convoy covered a considerable amount of ocean and was composed of other liners including the *Empress of Canada*, *Empress of Russia*, *Dominion Monarch* and *Narkunda*, and a sizeable escort. This included, from time to time, an 'R' class battleship (*Ramillies* or *Resolution*), the *Repulse*, the old aircraft carrier *Argus* and the cruisers *Devonshire* and *Dorsetshire*. There was also a mixed bag of destroyers; the ancient *Verity*, *Witch*, *Wrestler* and *Whitehall*, the equally ancient ex-American *Beverley* and *Stanley* and the Canadian *Assiniboine*. We used to pass the time trying to read the signals passed between the ships and I was very pleased when (with some help from one of our signallers) I was able to read orders to one of the destroyers to proceed to the Azores to refuel. Whilst we were in the North Atlantic there was not much they could do with us. We had PT every other day when there was space available on deck, lectures mainly on regimental history and, for some unearthly reason, frequent kit inspections. I can't remember where we found the space to lay out our kit. In the evenings there was invariably a housey-housey session (they call it bingo now).

After five days we were reported to be 1,000 miles west of Cape Finisterre at 25° west, 43° north and it started to get warmer so we were able to spend more time on deck and also to use the swimming pool. The warmer it got, the hotter it was down below, and most of us used to go up and sleep on deck, which was a great improvement; every square inch of deck was occupied. The only snag was that the first task of the crew was to wash down the deck, so we were woken early to shouts of 'wakey wakey, washy decky' followed, unless one was quick, by a jet of water from a hose.

After two weeks we pulled into Freetown, where we spent the next five days at anchor, surrounded by small boats manned by young boys selling fruit etc. and shouting 'Glasgae Tanner, boss' (the Glasgae Tanner was the old silver threepenny bit). If a coin – silver, not copper – was thrown into the water, they would dive in and catch it before it reached the bottom. I bought some bananas. About the only activities on board were PT and a tug of war competition and I spent two days as mess orderly, getting and clearing away the meals. The food was not too bad considering the numbers they had to cope with and there was quite a good canteen. As they were regularly on the run they were able to stock up in South Africa and had plenty of cigarettes including C to C (Cape to Cairo) and Springbok brands as well as chocolate and, I remember, melon and lemon jam which I took a fancy to. We left Freetown on 19 October in a somewhat smaller convoy of 23 ships with the Dorsetshire as our main escort and spent the next eleven days steaming south. I spent five days on a Bren gun cadre course (elementary stuff) and two days on semaphore before we arrived at Cape Town on the 30th.

After being cooped up on board for five weeks, the sight of Table Mountain looming on the horizon was very welcome. We docked at 6.30 in the evening and somewhat to our surprise we were allowed ashore at 9 pm for a couple of hours in time for a quick walk round and visit to a canteen. Next morning we went for a short route march but it took some time to get our shore legs again. We were allowed off at midday and were amazed to find masses of cars lined up at the dock gates manned by ladies of the South African Women's Auxiliary Services (a sort of WVS) who whisked everyone off to various canteens where after a brief stop for refreshments everyone was again picked up. We were taken to a beautiful old Dutch house, Newlands, for tea. The house was owned by a Mrs Thompson whose husband had been an officer in the Rifle Brigade. More ladies then turned up to take us off again. Three of us, Stan Haywood our platoon signaller, Tom Gray, who lost an eye at Medenine, and I were taken by Mrs Griffiths to her home in Plumstead where we met her husband, two small daughters (Geraldine and Margaret) and Hamish the Scottie dog. We had dinner and a chat and they took us back to the ship at about midnight.

Next morning there was a ceremonial march through Cape Town, with the salute being taken by the South African general commanding in Cape Province. So far as we were concerned it was a bit of a shambles because we were trying to march at riflemen's pace without treading on the heels of the 9th Lancers who were ahead of us, so we spent half the time marking time. Then as we approached the saluting base we found the South Africans had kindly supplied a band to play us past so we had to slow down and march past in a 'swashbuckling' style. We again got ashore at midday and this time we were taken by Mrs Griffiths' sister, Helen Carter, and her husband, to Stellenbosch for a *braai vleis* (meat barbecue) and again we got back to the ship at midnight. The following day we went ashore for lunch in Cape Town and then got the train to Plumstead and were taken for a drive around the area to Fishhoek, Kommetjie and the botanical gardens before spending the evening with them.

There was another short route march the following morning (they were determined to get our legs working again) after which we had a look round the shops and were then taken by the Griffiths to the beach at Muizenberg, followed by a dinner dance at Wynberg. This was our last run ashore so we had to say goodbye to them with much regret and many expressions of thanks. They had given us a marvellous time and had made us very much at home and we even managed to have a bath at their house, which was very welcome, as we had to wash in salt water on the ship. After we had gone they wrote to our families to let them know they had seen us and that we were well (a breach of security). It was not that we were exceptionally lucky, as all the other troops aboard received similar treatment. I don't know how the people of Cape Town managed it with convoys coming in every three or four weeks. In all they looked after more than a million troops from 46 convoys between July 1940 and October 1945. For the unlucky ones, especially those bound for Malaya, it was the last bit of enjoyment they ever had.

We sailed first thing on the morning of 4 November and on the 7th we arrived in Durban where the other half of the convoy had been spending the time. We had faint hopes of getting ashore again but after spending the night at anchor we docked in the morning and sailed again at teatime, escorted by *Repulse* which was soon to be sunk off Malaya. All we saw of Durban was the 'Lady in White', a lady named Perla Gibson, who used to stand on the end of the pier and sing to all the troops as the ships pulled out of the harbour. The Navy later put up a memorial to her on the pier.

The first week at sea I spent as mess orderly as we steamed up the east coast of Africa, then I had a week's signalling course learning how to operate the wireless set and all the procedures etc. so that I could take over a set if needed. This only ever happened once, when someone rushed up and said the sets were due to be 'netted' (tuned in to the right frequency) in five minutes and our signaller had gone off to the WC. I rushed over and manned the set but couldn't get a peep out of it and finally gave up in disgust. Just then the signaller returned and when I told him he just opened the battery box, which proved to be empty as the battery had been taken off for charging. It took a fortnight to get to Aden and we remained at anchor in the harbour there for five days, either because the Luftwaffe had been mining the Gulf of Suez or, more likely, until the Egyptian ports were clear. They liked to get the ships in and out as quickly as possible because of the periodic bombing raids. I continued my signal course but we did have one trip round the harbour in the ship's lifeboats which gave some amusement, as they were propelled by paddles which we operated by pulling levers to and fro in a pumping action. Being November it was reasonably cool as we set off through the Red Sea, passing the *Queen Elizabeth* on her way south probably after delivering ANZAC troops. We arrived at Port Tewfik, near Suez, three days later, at midday on 28 November.

The Desert –
From Arrival to Gazala

෴

We landed by tender and as we came ashore there were some Rifle Brigade officers waiting to greet us. One of them shouted, 'Welcome to the Middle East, but I'm afraid you're too late, it's all over. Rommel has only fourteen tanks left.' As it transpired he was speaking eighteen months too soon and Rommel was at that moment creating mayhem in the 8th Army's ten-day-old offensive as it was trying to link up with the Tobruk garrison.

Anyway, we spent a cold night in the train and found ourselves next morning at Amriya, on the fringe of the desert west of Alexandria. We were driven out to a patch of desert called Ikingi where we pitched tents and started sorting ourselves out whilst waiting for the vehicles to be unloaded from the Clan Campbell. There was nothing around – just a dusty and stony landscape with a NAAFI tent 'in the next desert', which we were able to visit after being paid. There was a considerable shortage of change, with the result that two men were given one banknote (100 piastres = £1) to share between them, so they had to stick together until they could start spending it in the NAAFI. Even there, small change was equally scarce so one was likely to receive a packet of chewing gum and three boiled sweets as part of one's change. The glasses there were all cut down from beer bottles and Stella was the usual brand. I believe the method used was to soak a piece of string in petrol, tie it around the bottle and set it alight, whereupon it cracked with a clean break. We managed to get into Alex for one day and have a bath, a meal and a look round. As it was winter and fairly cold we were in battledress and had to hand in our tropical uniforms. These had never been worn and we cursed the time we had spent at Swindon laboriously sewing scores of black buttons on the tunics. Our solar topees were piled in a heap and a couple of locals jumped up and down on them to squash them flat. They were never worn in the desert and why they were always issued to all the troops when they left England we never could tell. Our kitbags and any surplus kit were handed in and we had just the one battledress and what we could carry in our packs, plus two blankets and a groundsheet. When the vehicles arrived they had to be checked over and loaded, and all our weapons checked. We had one exercise practising moving across the desert and then we were ready to go.

December 1941

    As you can see we've arrived in the Middle East at last, and I can't say I'm very impressed by it. It seems to consist mainly of sand – at least that's all I've seen of it so far. At the moment we're under canvas in a sort of sea of sand, which gets in one's eyes, nose, mouth and ears, and also in all our kit, clothes, weapons and food. Moreover we've had to discard our tropical kit and get back to serge again, as it's fairly cold during the day, and almost freezing at night.

The company moved out by road on 13 December, a fortnight after arrival, but the carriers were going by rail to save wear on their tracks, so we stayed behind for another two days before leaving in a rush one afternoon. We spent the night out on the flat trucks with the carriers and arrived at Mersa Matruh the following morning. After unloading and getting some breakfast at the transit camp, we set off down the Siwa track travelling about 40 miles southwest to El Kanayis where we rejoined the company. Two days later, on 18 December, we set off westwards to catch up with the 8th Army, who by then had joined up with the Tobruk garrison and pushed on as far as Gazala, where Rommel had just turned and had a swipe at part of the Indian Division. Much closer at hand, German garrisons were still holding out on the Egypt–Libya border at Halfaya Pass and nearby Bardia, so it was not possible to move forward all the way by the coast road, which was the only paved road in the country. In any event we needed to go via the desert in order to get used to the conditions and practice moving as a brigade in desert formation.

There was a lot of desert ahead of us. From Alexandria to Mersa Matruh was 150 miles and to Sollum on the Libyan border, 300. Tobruk was nearly 400 miles, Benghazi 675 miles and El Agheila, the limit of advance until 1943, was 850. Tripoli, the German/Italian base and ultimate goal, was 500 miles further on. The farther one side advanced, the more stretched its line of supply became and the fewer troops it could maintain in the forward area. The enemy became correspondingly stronger as his lines of communication got shorter, until eventually he was able to turn to the offensive himself. This was the reason for the up and down nature of the campaign, added to which it was essentially a war of movement. There were few places where it was possible to make a stand without being outflanked and therefore once one had started running, one had to carry on until the opposition ran out of breath.

Most of the fighting took place in the 700 mile stretch between Matruh and Agheila and within 30 miles of the coast except in the Jebel Akhdar, the fertile and hilly area in the bulge of coast between Derna and Benghazi. This was unsuitable for mobile forces who therefore used to cut across the desert inland. The ground was more often stony than sandy but always with a thin covering of sand to blow around. There were places where the sand was loose and soft, causing vehicles to get stuck and have to be dug out, usually with the help of sand channels. These places would become quagmires after one of the infrequent rainstorms. In other places it was flat and firm and we could race across at full tilt with hardly a jolt. The salt pans, however, could be dangerous because they had a firm crust which, if too thin, gave way causing the vehicle to sink into the bog underneath. The traditional sand dunes were generally only found close to the seashore or much further south towards the Sahara. Apart from the coast road there were no metalled roads, only a few Senussi camel tracks such as the Trigh el Abd and Trigh Capuzzo running east and west and the tracks running south to the oases of Siwa and Lalo. Nor were there any permanent settlements away from the coast and the Jebel. The few Senussi lived in tents with their small herds of goats and camels and moved around according to the availability of water. The place names on the maps were mainly Birs (wells), Sidis (tombs of holy men, marked by a few stones), Qarats (rises in the ground) and Ghots or Deirs (depressions). Birs generally held water only after rain and then only enough for the Senussi and their animals, not for large armies. Generally speaking there were no obstacles to driving in any direction, except near the coast where in many places there were a series of escarpments which were not always negotiable when moving from north to south or vice versa.

Traffic in the rear area tended to follow the main tracks but these became very cut up with clouds of sand billowing up behind every vehicle. People therefore moved to one side in search of firmer going with the result that the tracks became wider and wider. We moved around by compass. This meant periodically getting out of the vehicle and walking far enough away to avoid any magnetic attraction before taking a bearing, hopefully to some recognisable object on the skyline. This might be a cairn or crashed aircraft which we would then drive towards before repeating the process. We never felt in any danger from the desert itself. There was no question of dying of thirst or starvation if stranded, because one always knew that by walking north for twenty miles or so (preferably at night when it was cool and the stars were there to guide) one would meet somebody eventually, even if it was the enemy. No one I knew ever did get forced to walk, except for those who got caught by a German advance and deliberately chose to walk back (often with help from the Senussi) rather than give themselves up. There was little vegetation other than the odd patch of camel scrub, except after rain when many small flowers would spring up and bloom for a short while. There was a certain amount of wildlife including jerboas, the occasional gazelle, snakes and scorpions. Generally speaking the Senussi were on our side, mainly because of the Italian habit before the war of dropping rebel chieftains out of aeroplanes without the benefit of parachutes.

The two great bugbears were sand and flies. On the move every vehicle threw up a cloud of sand and even though they were spaced well apart, the air was full of it and goggles and eye-shields were needed if one wanted to keep one's eyes open. Driving at night, closed up, was far worse because one was driving straight into a cloud of dust and, occasionally, straight into an unseen slit trench or into the vehicle in front if it stopped suddenly! When stationary, if there was any sort of breeze the sand used to blow with it, getting into everything. Worst of all was the Khamsin wind. One could see this great black cloud right across the horizon, rapidly getting nearer until suddenly one was engulfed in a gale of sand which nothing could keep out. It brought everything to a standstill until it had passed over. Luckily it was not very frequent, but even the ordinary movement around the desert seemed to leave our faces permanently caked with a layer of 'pancake' make-up. Flies, I think, were even more irritating than sand, certainly when one was eating or resting during the day. One could understand their being around in areas that had been occupied by troops, or where battles had been fought, but one could pull up in what appeared to be virgin desert, never before visited by man, and within two minutes the flies would arrive. They were most persistent when food and drink were about and we used to cut the top off a tin (a sausage tin was the best size) to use as a lid for our mugs, but even in the moment it took to raise the lid and take a swig, two or three flies would manage to get in and drown themselves. With a plate of food, people would get up and dash off in different directions hoping (without success) to leave the flies behind. Trying to rest in the heat of the day, one was either kept awake brushing off the flies or kept awake sweltering under a blanket or coat, which we put over our heads to keep them off.

During the winter it was quite cool and we wore battledress, with greatcoats and balaclavas at night. The officers in the Guards Brigade had a fancy for long, ankle-length sheepskin coats, which made them look rather like Mongolians and not very much like a Buckingham Palace guard. During the summer the normal dress was boots, socks and shorts – the shorts preferably considerably shortened from the 'official' length. Once we were acclimatised there was no problem with sunburn nor with sunstroke, proving how unnecessary were the topees and spine-pads of an earlier generation. We wore side-caps or 'cap comforters' – a woollen rectangle of double thickness which, when one half was folded into the other, turned into a hat rather like a pirate's. This was less likely to fall off than a side-cap, which was a ridiculous garment. Tin hats, as we insisted on calling steel helmets in defiance of the orders of High Command, who thought it cast doubts on their efficiency, were only worn when shot and shell were flying around. In similar vein, we were discouraged from calling the enemy 'Jerry' because it sounded too friendly – he was supposed to be called the Hun or the Bosche, but never was. Desert sores were a nuisance. Small knocks or cuts never seemed to heal up but kept on festering and were of course an area of attraction for the flies, so our arms and legs were often festooned with bits of grubby bandage in an attempt to keep them off.

Rations were pretty basic and not overgenerous, particularly when we were advancing and getting farther away from the supply dumps. Basically it was one tin of bully beef or M&V (meat and veg) plus two packets of biscuits per man per day. In addition there was a bit of tinned bacon (largely fat which melted away when fried, leaving a few shreds of lean) or sausage (later it was usually soya links, which were cordially disliked as they tasted like sawdust). From time to time we also got tinned fruit, potatoes, cheese, margarine and marmalade or jam. We also got enough sugar and evaporated milk for the amount of tea we could drink with the water available.

'Breaking bulk' was always a problem with rations. Our vehicles were always dispersed in the desert, 100 to 150 yards apart, to minimise the risk from bombing or shelling and because we were liable to be sent off in different directions, as well as the risk of breakdown, etc., it was essential that the rations for the crew were distributed to each vehicle. With the carriers we had a crew of three and later, with the anti-tank guns, six at full strength. But the platoon might get 2 lb tins of margarine, sausages, jam etc., and it was impracticable to open the tins and split the food up, as it was too difficult to keep it in reasonable condition. So we used to take turns, taking a complete tin and making it last until one's turn came round again. This worked well once the system was in full operation but at first it meant going short of some things for a while. We sometimes got porridge oats, rice or flour, but rarely had enough water to make use of them. The first time we got up to El Agheila, rations were pretty short, almost down to the basic bully and biscuits, and not even our 50-a-week cigarette ration came up. Then for several months we were not too far from Tobruk and supplies became better. They even sent us fresh meat and bread sometimes but most of the former went off before it got to us and the bread was stale and mouldy. On occasion they also gave us dried potatoes and greens but again it was a question of having enough water. We had a free issue of 50 cigarettes a week, and hopefully could get another 50 through the NAAFI. The former were usually the unpopular 'V for Victory' or the even more disliked 'Green V', made in India. I used to smoke my pipe at first, but apart from the difficulty of getting tobacco, my pipes kept getting broken when I was bouncing around in the carrier until they were bound up with so much adhesive tape that smoke was coming out from everywhere and I had to give up and stick to cigarettes. We relied very much on parcels from home, which took between four and seven months to arrive so one had to be patient when told that one was on its way.

Water was very short, especially in the early stages. Our carriers were equipped with three 2-gallon cans which was theoretically a gallon a man a day for two days. The cans sometimes got holed by stones flung up by the tracks, the radiator sometimes needed topping up, and we had to keep some in reserve in case the water truck, as sometimes happened, failed to turn up, so effectively we had about half a gallon a head for drinking, cooking and washing. Once we got wise, we started collecting 'Jerricans' holding about five gallons each from abandoned German vehicles, and using them instead gave us a much better supply. Also, as our people got more desert-wise, they would get wind of a Bir where there was water and a truck would be sent with all the cans to be filled.

Breakfast was normally a bit of sausage or bacon, biscuits and marmalade, and tea. At midday a bully and biscuit sandwich or sometimes cheese, and tea. The evening meal was meat and veg, or fried or stewed bully with tinned fruit if there was any. Then, water permitting, we occasionally had 'biscuit burgoo' which was made by crushing biscuits into powder (like porridge oats), mixing in water, heating it up and eating with evaporated milk and sugar or syrup. Additional 'brews' of tea depended on the availability of water and opportunity. We cooked with petrol and I think we used nearly as much petrol for cooking as for moving around. There was a big row once when someone on the staff worked out how many thousands of gallons were being used in the division every day at a time when we were not moving but there was no alternative. When we first went out we had a petrol cooker on the carrier but it took about an hour to boil enough water for tea before we started cooking anything, and anyway the jets kept getting clogged with sand and we soon ran out of prickers. It was left on our carrier when we dumped it and never replaced. There was no wood lying about for fuel so we used to cut a four-gallon petrol tin in half, half fill it with sand, pour in a generous amount of petrol and light up. We put the water in a similar half petrol tin, put it in the fire and waited for it to boil. We also used petrol tins as cooking pots, unless we had managed to find anything more suitable on one of the many abandoned vehicles in the desert. The 8th Army on the move looked like a gang of gypsy tinkers, with sooty pots and pans hanging from all the vehicles. To lose one's brew can was a disaster until one could get another one. The thin petrol tins were themselves a disaster because many of them sprang a leak on the long bumpy journey from the railhead, and it is estimated that half the petrol was lost in this way. It is strange that the British Army provided no cooking equipment of any sort for the mobile units. The infantry battalions had company cooks with cookers, dixies, etc. who cooked the meals, which were then taken up to the troops in hayboxes and eaten half-cold. We had them too when we started but the cooks and their equipment went into the bag on the first day in action and were never replaced. They were in any case of no use to us as we were often miles away. It was the same in Europe, using earth instead of sand, although it was sometimes possible to use wood or to get into a house and use their solid fuel cooker.

We aimed to make and drink a brew in fifteen minutes, although it was sometimes a bit tight as the tea was slow to cool in the heat. When on the move there were always unexplained halts which might last five minutes or five hours and if we were thirsty there was always temptation to risk a brew. Sometimes permission was officially granted (we had a flag signal for that) but even that was no guarantee that we would not move at any minute. Luckily we had a large thermos into which we could pour the brew if someone shouted 'blue flag up' and all across the desert people could be seen frantically dousing their fires and hitching red-hot brew-cans on to their vehicles.

The shortage of water meant that its use for washing was kept to a minimum. Half a pint was normal for a shave and wash and anything left probably went into the radiator. I did try once straining it through pebbles to drink but it was not a success. At one time water was so short that I went a fortnight without a wash and shave – I found the sand made the beard very itchy. There were odd occasions when we were able to have a good washdown either when things were quiet and there was a well not far away or when we had been able to collect some rainwater. We washed clothes when necessary (mainly shirts and socks) in petrol as it was so much more plentiful than water.

The brigade set off a week before Christmas, moving as usual in regimental groups. This meant that each of the three tank regiments had attached to it a battery of field guns, a motor company from our battalion (with three infantry platoons and a scout platoon in carriers) plus a troop of anti-tank guns and one of Bofors light AA guns. These all moved in open formation covering miles of desert and looking very much like a fleet at sea. Later, when we became an anti-tank company, each of our platoons went with a different regimental group so we were even more split up. Working like this, one saw more of the people from other units in the same group than one did of those in one's own battalion, but in any case, with vehicles so widely dispersed, for most of the time it was just three or six of us together. It was important that people should be able to get on well without getting on one another's nerves – generally it worked remarkably well and there was very little friction. At night we went into 'close leaguer' with the vehicles closed up nose to tail in half a dozen or more columns; this was so that control could be exercised in any emergency such as an attack or

Christmas Dinner 1941 – Bir Gibni

sudden move. If the vehicles had remained dispersed a hundred yards or more apart it would have been impossible to pass on any orders in the darkness. We had to open out again at first light to avoid becoming an easy target for any enemy within range.

We did about 50 miles a day for three days, passing through the wire marking the Egyptian-Libyan border at Bir Sheferzen and leaguering at Bir Gibni. We had our first sandstorm just before we got there and in the middle of it, miles from anywhere, we suddenly bumped into a mobile canteen. It gave us an unduly favourable impression of the desert because we hardly ever saw another canteen. What it was doing there I don't know but we were very glad of it because our B Echelon seemed to be having some difficulty in finding its way round the desert and failed to arrive with the rations for two days.

We stayed at Bir Gibni for nine days, which we spent doing maintenance and testing as well as cleaning weapons and practising exercises with the tanks. Christmas Day was the same as any other except that there was a church parade instead of work – otherwise it was just bully and biscuits. We set off again, north-east this time, late on the 29th and by the night of the 30th had travelled about 80 miles through the area where some of the previous month's battles had taken place. This brought us to Bir Aslagh, about 25 miles southwest of Tobruk and close to the cross tracks which became known as 'Knightsbridge'. This was an area with which we were to become all too familiar in the fighting five months later. We stayed here another five days due to a shortage of petrol, a tanker having been sunk on its way into Tobruk. On 4 January we were off again, cutting across the desert south of the Jebel for 180 miles, some of it through very difficult rocky country. Part of it was littered with Italian Thermos bombs which had been dropped from aircraft, which looked like Thermos flasks and went off when they were moved. On the third day we reached Antelat, about 60 miles south of Benghazi, where we sat down again for what eventually turned out to be twelve days before we finally moved up to relieve our 2nd Battalion.

January 1942

The weather is still fine though rather cold. We have had no news, except about the local situation, for some time. Pay comes up rather irregularly and so do the canteen stocks, so it always seems to happen that when you've got plenty of money there's nothing to spend it on, and when there's plenty of stuff to buy, there's no money to buy it with!

We cut one another's hair the other day with my nail scissors and a razor! I won't say it looks exactly professional, but at least it got the worst off, though it is rather cold round the ears.

The other day we did a bit of digging but were forced to give it up until they decide to issue us with pneumatic drills. Talk about rock, I got enough out of my hole alone to make a crazy paving path long enough to go two or three times round our garden.

Forgive scrawl, but what with sandy ink sandy paper and sandy me, to say nothing of a fifteen mph breeze, I'm afraid it's the best I can do.

The army was in great difficulty, as it had been twelve months previously. The Germans had wrecked and mined the port of Benghazi before they left and all our supplies had to come from Tobruk, more than 400 miles away by road, or even from railheads in

Egypt more than 500 miles away. The more troops they kept in the line facing Rommel, the more supplies they needed and the longer it would take to build up dumps of supplies for the next stage of the advance to Tripoli. They therefore kept the force to the minimum, whilst grounding the rest of the army and using its transport to help on the supply line. The 7th Armoured Division were holding the line but their armoured brigade had already been withdrawn, as it had only twenty tanks left out of about 180 and they were worn out. It consisted only of the support group (two motor battalions and a regiment of artillery) plus the Guards Brigade (two battalions and a field regiment) with a couple of armoured car regiments. We in the 1st Armoured Division were to relieve the 7th, but our armoured brigade was to remain back at Antelat as there was not enough petrol for them to operate forward and in any case the tanks were in need of repair and maintenance after their 1,000-mile journey across the desert. The Crusader was notorious for being mechanically unreliable and anyone following the brigade across the desert could do so with ease by making his way from one broken-down tank to another. This was not a great problem when advancing but when withdrawing every broken-down tank was a loss either blown up or captured by the enemy. I think more tanks were lost in this way than were actually hit in battle. We were on very low rations by this time and instead of our normal cigarette issue they gave us twenty Italian cigarettes and ten cigars from stocks captured in Benghazi; after a couple of puffs we decided to go without. At least we got our first mail since leaving home; my first two letters had been posted in October, three months before.

We finally set off on 18 January, moving forward 85 miles over two days. The platoon commander told us that four columns were to be formed, with the KRRC (Kings Royal Rifle Corps) and ourselves each providing two companies. This meant that two companies would remain in reserve and the company commanders had tossed up to see which should go forward. Unfortunately we had lost. A rifleman: 'You mean we've got to go up?' Platoon commander: 'No, we lost so we have to stay in reserve.' The area in which we were to operate was one of very soft sand in which the armoured cars, which were also worn out, kept getting stuck. As a result it was decided to send up the carrier platoons of the two companies in reserve to replace them. So we left the rest of the company and went forward another 40 miles, through country much more Saharan in appearance, to a hill called Mount Betafel and down into the Wadi Faregh. Next morning, the 21st, we joined our column, which was named 'James' after our colonel. We were at last 'up the sharp end', on the very day that Rommel chose to attack. He had been in difficulty with his supplies because a naval force of cruisers and destroyers based in Malta, known as Force K, had been getting amongst his convoys from Italy to Tripoli, but unfortunately one night they ran into a minefield. Three cruisers and a destroyer were sunk or damaged and that was the end of Force K, so Rommel was able to get another 50 tanks, plus guns, men and petrol through.

We had only just arrived when, looking north, we saw a lot of vehicles moving rapidly eastwards along the top of the escarpment, then there was a gap followed by another lot of vehicles. Our guns opened fire on this second group, from which we deduced that they were German. Our own tanks were over a hundred miles back, so we had no option but to scarper if we were not to be left behind. Our section of three carriers was sent off northwards to try to find out what was going on, but before doing so we had our first experience of Stukas. These had been transferred from the Russian Front to help Rommel – it must have been a change of temperature for them. The noise was quite frightening but with vehicles well-dispersed the damage was usually slight, particularly in soft sand. On this occasion one vehicle, C Company's Officers' Mess truck, was destroyed (loud laughter from the troops) and our platoon 'mother truck' which carried stores etc. was damaged but no one was hurt. I found myself hiding behind a small piece of camel scrub, creeping round to keep it between me and the Stukas, though I don't think they were taking that degree of personal interest in me. When we rejoined the column after our patrol we found that C Company had only one of their eleven carriers left and two of ours had had to be dumped because of breakdowns.

We set off eastwards again at dawn next morning. The going was very soft and vehicles kept getting stuck and two more of our carriers broke down and had to be dumped. We went off on patrol but lost radio touch and went back 50 miles before we eventually raised them and found they were at El Haselat, twenty miles north-north-east of us. Next morning the column moved off again but we had to remain behind for petrol to arrive. Luckily Jerry must have stopped for breakfast too, because we were on the move again before his armoured cars came in sight and started chasing us. We tried to keep them at a distance with our Brens and eventually caught up with one of our other columns and joined them on a night march to Saunnu well. Rommel was by now well ahead of us and there were Very Lights from their leaguers going up all round us. They always advertised their presence with lights – we always kept dark and silent. The Italians were even known to have a couple of motorcyclists riding round and round their leaguers, very useful to our patrols if they wanted to get close in without being heard. We caught up with our tanks again at Saunnu – they had been in action that day and two of the regiments had suffered severely. One had only eight tanks left out of over 60, but as usual there were more losses from breakdowns than from anything else. We spent the day there, shelling and being shelled by German tanks, and being on the receiving end of several Stuka raids. Next morning we went out to recce the German positions and picked up a couple of prisoners in a truck that had gone astray – the first Germans we had seen. We were soon chased away by tanks and made off northwards towards Msus (Maisus), being shelled and bombed along the way. Msus was the location of our main petrol dump but Rommel got there before we did and the people in charge blew it up. There was a 40-mile journey ahead of us and whilst we had enough petrol for our carriers other vehicles were very short so it was decided to dump our carriers (which did only about three miles to the gallon) and use the petrol for the trucks.

We were very upset at losing our carrier, which had never let us down in our long trek across the desert. It was named the Three Virgins because the crew – Nobby Mewstone, Bert Bolton and I – were all bachelors. Its motto was 'Benghazi or bust' – actually it did both. I was co-opted into a plot by Sergeant Mulford to hide until everyone had gone and then make off in his carrier, but someone blew the gaff and it was scrubbed – probably just as well. We could not set fire to our carriers nor put a sledgehammer to them because it would have given our position away, so we had to content ourselves with filling the sump with sand. We planned to booby-trap the toolbox with a hand grenade, but luckily someone stopped us. Some weeks later Nobby Mewstone, our carrier commander, managed to bump into his brother who was in the Royals, an armoured car regiment. He said to Nobby 'I've been looking for you, I wish you wouldn't leave your rubbish all over the desert' and handed back his driving licence which had been left with some of his kit on the carrier. They had been patrolling in the area, by then miles behind the German lines, and come across our carriers.

We climbed on the three-tonners with just our weapons and what we could carry in our haversacks. I handed up my Boyes anti-tank rifle but somebody rapidly pitched it overboard – it was quite useless against tanks anyway. We drove continuously through the night north to Charruba, dodging German leaguers on the way. Here we met more of our platoon and some others from the company and temporarily formed ourselves into two motor platoons sharing a three-tonner. We took up defence positions for three days while we sorted ourselves out. Luckily Jerry had not followed us up but had turned towards Benghazi and didn't have the resources to come across the desert as well. Here we started to find out what had happened to the rest of the company. We had had to dump four of our carriers with breakdowns (but the crews were all picked up) and had left five behind at Msus. Two were missing with their crews and we later heard that all six were prisoners. One crew was on patrol with Goldie Millar, the commander of C Company carrier platoon. He later escaped from prison camp, made contact with the French Resistance and eventually got back home. He parachuted back into France and joined the Maquis, writing a couple of books about it. The other carrier had broken down earlier and was with the rest of the company when they got themselves caught by a

German column. About half of Company HQ went 'into the bag', including the company commander and second-in-command with half of 7 Platoon and a section of 6. About 46 from the company were taken prisoner in all – about 25–30% of its compliment. Luckily only one man was killed and about four wounded, but unfortunately two of the prisoners were later drowned when one of our subs torpedoed the ship taking them to Italy. One of the other companies also had quite a number taken prisoner and the battalion lost about a hundred in all. The second-in-command, Major Vic Turner (who later won the VC at Alamein when commanding the 2nd Battalion) and several others started walking when they lost their truck, but decided they'd never make it on foot. So they kept watch beside a track until a German staff car came along. A couple of them lay down and pretended to be in a bad way and when the car slowed they bundled the officers out and drove off, eventually landing up in Tobruk.

We moved back from Charruba to Mechili and then south to Tengeder, then back to various positions in what was to become the Gazala Line. After a fortnight they told us we were to be turned into an anti-tank company. Until then anti-tank guns had been manned by the Royal Artillery but it was thought that the infantry, as well as needing more protection from tanks, might be more comfortable than the gunners at the very short ranges needed to knock out German tanks. We took two days to drive back to Matruh to collect the 2-pounders and learn how to use them, but after messing about there for five days they decided to do it at Tobruk, so we had to drive all the way back again.

We were actually about twenty miles beyond Tobruk and they gave us a number of marquees to put up, but before we had even finished we found the disadvantage of the place. Every time the Stukas raided Tobruk the fighter escort used to come down low and streak westwards for home, strafing anything interesting they saw on the way, which included our tents. After four days of this they hit one of the officers still lying in his bed (we were in the breakfast queue, which rapidly dispersed) so they promptly decided to move us back within the Tobruk perimeter where the AA barrage would keep the Me's to a respectable height. We were in a nice little wadi right by the sea, so there were ample opportunities for bathes in the Med. Pat Sydes, who was later killed at Alamein, and I dug a nice deep hole, pitched our two man bivvy over the top, carved out sleeping places, shelves, etc., stuck a 'Mon Repos' sign outside and made ourselves comfortable – the most comfortable spot I had in the desert. After about a week we were duly declared proficient anti-tank gunners and went off back to the battalion with our 2-pounders.

February 1942

It's getting a bit warmer here now, a taste of pleasures to come no doubt! There's not much fresh news as life in the desert is very monotonous. We have lost track of the war completely out here, as we get no news at all, only stupendous rumours which are denied after about two days.

An unusual event which has occurred out here is that I've had a bath, or at least a shower bath. After months of washing in a mug full of water between three of us, it seemed very luxurious to stand there while about four trickles of lukewarm water fell down my back.

Working with the guns was quite exhausting. They were carried on the chassis of a 3-ton truck called a portee and could be fired from there, although this was not too popular in a pitched battle. It was no joke being perched four feet up in the air with no protection from shot or shell other than the gunshield. So the gun was winched down to the ground (and back up) along ramps which we placed at the back of the truck. Going down was easy, although if the chaps up top got too eager to get it done with they were liable to give too hearty a shove; the gun would come flying down the ramps and the chap on the winch handle would lose his grip. He would then have to duck rapidly in order to avoid getting a clout from the handle – language tended to get a bit ripe on these occasions. We then had to unload ammunition, Bren gun and rifles, digging tools, water and food, etc., and start digging. First a slit trench each – 6 feet long, 18 inches to 2 feet wide and as deep as energy, fear and rocky ground dictated. Then we had to dig the gunpit,

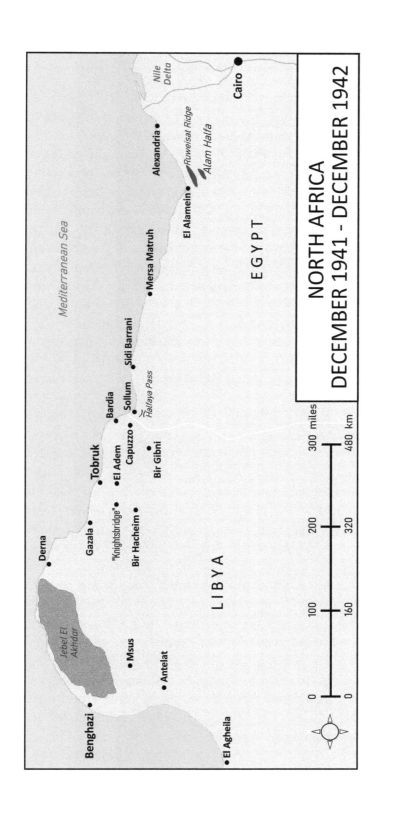

NORTH AFRICA
DECEMBER 1941 - DECEMBER 1942

Mediterranean Sea

Nile
Delta

Cairo

Alexandria

Ruweisat Ridge
Alam Halfa

El Alamein

Mersa Matruh

EGYPT

Sidi Barrani

Sollum
Bardia
Hafaya Pass

Tobruk
El Adem
Capuzzo
Bir Gibni

Derna

Gazala
"Knightsbridge"
Bir Hacheim

LIBYA

Jebel El
Akhdar

Msus

Antelat

Benghazi

El Agheila

0   100   200   300 miles
0   160   320   480 km

circular with a diameter of about 8 feet and about 18 inches deep. The gun was then pushed in and the wheels removed. Coming out of action, the wheels had first to be replaced with two men lifting each side of the gun in turn whilst a third replaced the wheel. Then the portee backed up to the pit and the eye on the trail was coupled up to the towing hook. We relied on accurate drivers to get it right first time with no messing about going back and forwards whilst Rommel was getting ever nearer. The gun was pulled out of the pit, ramps put down, gun winched up, wheels removed, ammunition and stores reloaded and off we went. It was like a mild version of the naval field gun competition at the Royal Tournament. Not too bad done once on a peaceful day, but having to do it several times a day, moving on almost as soon as one had finished digging (or sometimes before) and with the Afrika Korps trying to interfere with the process, was more than tiring. I am not sure of the weight of the 2-pounder but the 6-pounder was 7-cwt – about 800 pounds – which was quite a weight to heave around.

We were not all that happy with the 2-pounder because we needed to let German tanks come within about 400 yards before our shot would penetrate and in the absence of any cover in the desert they could usually see us long before and sit back and pot at us in safety. Our tanks suffered from the same problem. The German tanks' guns had twice the effective range of ours so our tanks had to rush forward, hoping that enough would survive to meet the panzers on equal terms when they got to close range. For this reason we welcomed getting the 6-pounders later on, as we could then take them on at 800 to 1000 yards, but it was a bigger and heavier gun and therefore more tiring to hump around. Its traverse was only about 30° instead of 360° (the wheels remained on) which meant that for any target outside the 30° the gun had to be physically manhandled, one man to each trail-leg and one to each wheel. As the trails dug themselves in after each shot it took quite a lot of effort to shift it. Furthermore, the gunpit had to be quite a lot bigger, about twice the diameter needed for the 2-pounder, which not only meant more digging, but also provided less protection for the crew.

March 1942

We have already covered several thousand miles of desert in our travels and are beginning to feel quite at home in it. The first sensation you get is one of miles and miles of nothingness, and you wonder how on earth anyone can find their way, but after a month or so you begin to get used to it and develop a sense of direction, so that you never feel lost.

No doubt you were rather worried not hearing for so long – I don't know what the news was like, but we were rather busy here! Thanks so much for sending the cigarettes and papers which I hope to see soon, we are still eagerly scanning any of last Octobers papers we can get hold of, so you can guess how rare they are ... We hope to start leave fairly soon, it only takes about fourteen months to go through the roster, so I may get some about next Christmas. They give you five clear days in town with about three days each way for travelling. It's not like being in England, but it makes a break from the desert anyway.

By the way, I wish Dad could see my hair now. Talk about a woolly sheep-dog, it needs a lawn mower not scissors. Still, it's just as good as cotton wool in the ears – keeps all the big bangs out. We had rice for dinner today, so it's a Red Letter Day – when I think how I used to be told to 'sit there till I do eat it' or 'one day you'll wish you hadn't left it on the plate'!

I'm afraid I can't say much as there is nothing to write that isn't censorable.

The next couple of months were quiet so far as contact with the enemy was concerned. The 8th Army was building up a series of defended localities known as boxes, protected by minefields, running south from Gazala. The Germans were on a line running south from Tmimi so there was about 30 miles of 'no-man's land' between the two armies into which Jock columns (consisting mainly of a battery of guns and one of our motor companies) ventured from time to time to see what trouble they could stir up. We were not called upon to participate and the only hostility we encountered was strafing from the odd bunch of Me's. Someone managed to shoot one down with a

Ken at Bir Gibni – April 1942

Bren gun one day, so they came back an hour later and dropped more bombs on us. But the powers that be kept us busy, even if Rommel didn't. Apart from the eternal gun drill (gun bumping we called it) and maintenance, there were battalion and brigade schemes and occasional alerts when a German column strayed too close to our part of the desert. The Duke of Gloucester came out to inspect us, so we even had an RSM's drill parade in preparation (luckily not also attended by the Luftwaffe) and they even took us on a couple of route marches across the desert. One day we drove twenty miles to the sea for a swim but on the way back a sandstorm blew up and it was 4 am before we got back, in a much worse state than we had been in before the swim.

Leave to Cairo and Alexandria was started but the war broke out again before my turn came round.

May 1942

It is still fairly warm out here and decidedly dry, especially when the Khamsin blows. I tried drinking soapy shaving water the other day but can't call the experiment a success! ...

... I had a banana yesterday, the first out here, about 3 inches long.

The Desert – The Gazala Line Battle and Retreat

∾⟨⟩∾

On 24 May we were put on alert, for the German attack was expected, but on the 25th some of us were sent down south to the Retma box, where our 2nd Battalion was in position, to get instruction from the Rhodesian anti-tank battery there on how to handle the 6-pounder guns which we were expecting to get shortly. Early on the morning of the 27th we abandoned our course and rushed back to our position, as the German attack had started. For reasons that I quite fail to understand (even after reading all the official and unofficial accounts since) the 8th Army was caught on the hop, even though the attack was expected. Rommel could either make a direct attack on the defended line running south from Gazala or he could circle round to the south and come up behind it. We in the 1st Armoured Division were concentrated behind the defended line towards the north, whilst the 7th Armoured Division were east of Bir Hacheim to block any right hook coming round the south. Our commanders for some reason were convinced that the attack would come in the centre. When our armoured cars reported that the Afrika Korps was on the move to the south they were convinced that it was a feint despite the armoured cars reporting half-hourly for 26 hours that large numbers of tanks were on the move. Although 7th Armoured Div. HQ were aware of these reports and in fact asked permission, which was refused, to move to their battle stations; they took no steps to warn their units to stand-to which was the least they should have done. Even when the 7th Motor Brigade reported that they were being chased by the Afrika Korps, Div. HQ thought that the brigadier (a rifleman as it happened) 'had the wind up'. In consequence the tank crews of the 4th Armoured Brigade were still washing and having a leisurely breakfast when the

German tanks appeared on the horizon. They had no time to get into battle positions and two of their regiments lost nearly all their tanks, whilst the Germans swept on to overrun Div. HQ. They captured the divisional commander, who took off his badges of rank, pretended to be a private and escaped the next day, but not before one of his German guards had commiserated with him for being a bit old to be 'sent up the desert'. The Germans next bumped the 22nd Armoured Brigade, who were part of 1st Armoured Division but standing by to go south to join the 7th if the attack came that way. Due to the confusion the order never came. They were having an even more leisurely breakfast and were apparently still in blissful ignorance of anything untoward going on and one of their regiments suffered severely. The loss of Div. HQ meant that the three brigades, already considerably disorganised, were wandering around without getting any orders, whilst Corps and Army HQ were getting no information about where they were and what was happening. It was a bad start to the Gazala action from which we never really recovered.

May 1942

> *The first parcel of cigarettes arrived on the 25th, they were undamaged and quite fresh. I'm sorry I haven't been able to answer sooner but as you no doubt know by now Rommel is up to his larks again and we are kept fairly active …*
>
> *… I can't imagine what it would be like to be home now – sitting in the garden in the shade with a nice cool drink – finding shade in the desert is more difficult than finding a mouse in a cat's home.*

Meanwhile we were driving back to our positions with the 2nd Armoured Brigade, surrounded by flocks of 3-tonners going flat out across the desert – all the signs of a typical 'flap'. The battle over the coming days was, I think, the worst in which I was engaged during the war, because it went on continuously for about three weeks and was so physically exhausting. Most of the action took place in an area about twenty miles by fifteen southwest of Tobruk which became known as the Cauldron (short for Devil's Cauldron). This area was west of El

Adem and east of our minefields and in it we went round and round in circles, moving several times a day. Each time we had to dig in, often under shellfire which was sometimes very heavy, especially when we had to pull out at the last moment. If our tanks were ordered to withdraw they just pulled back through us and made off, but we had to wait until our trucks came up, loaded up, hooked up the guns, etc., whilst the German tanks were getting uncomfortably close. The movement of hundreds of tanks and thousands of trucks, coupled with all the shelling, meant that there was usually a heavy dust cloud over the area – literally the 'fog of war'. Moreover, being midsummer, the days were at their longest and the nights shortest. It was after 10 pm before we could safely pull into leaguer and we had to be up again at about 4 am to open out at dawn. In the meantime we had to wait for replenishment – petrol, water, rations and ammunition – which was sometimes late arriving. We also had to deal with any repairs etc. and get orders. The rest of the night we could sleep except for our turn on guard or listening post. Even then the Luftwaffe took a hand. One plane would come droning up, circle round once and drop a flare which always seemed designed to light us up personally. As he came around for the third time we would dart for the nearest slit trench, only to find that he was dropping anti-personnel bombs which burst above the ground. So we would then dash back and crawl under the truck, but soon learned that on his fourth circuit he would drop high explosive. They rarely hit very much, but it was hard to convince oneself that there was not much danger. The engines always seemed to have a lighter note when they had dropped their load and we could hear the plane drone off westwards and settle down to sleep again, only to hear the next one coming up to repeat the process a few minutes later. After some days of this, one could be in a slit trench with shells landing all around, keeping an anxious eye on the sun to see if it was really getting any nearer to the horizon and wondering whether one would still be around to see the sunset and just drop off to sleep. Actually, lying in a slit trench one was relatively safe; shells could burst almost on the lip without doing any harm except to one's nerves. One night in leaguer I woke up to find the track of a tank across the very bottom of my groundsheet. Luckily I must have had my legs tucked up. It was one of our 'lame ducks' that came in late after a breakdown and cut it rather fine.

After a few days of this I got an unexpected break. We were in position somewhere in the Bir Harmat-Bir Aslagh area and had no time to dig a gun pit whilst the brigade was trying unsuccessfully to push the Afrika Korps back into the minefields. The 10th Hussars finished the day with three tanks, having started the battle with 60. There was a German tank about 1,000 yards in front, hull down. I was sitting in the layer's seat and could see him in my sights, but at that range it was pointless to fire at him. Suddenly everything went black. The next I remember was the voice of the company commander, who happened to be visiting our gun at the time, saying 'Move him into that slit trench, we'll have to bury him later', whereupon I sat up and said 'Not bloody likely' or words to that effect. What had happened was that the tank had fired a solid (armour piercing) shot which had come through our gun shield and caught the top of my tin hat, giving it a dent about two inches long and an inch deep, but not penetrating it. A splinter from the gun shield had cut my knuckles but I was otherwise undamaged, although I had been pitched out of my layer's seat onto the ground and knocked out for a second. I was somewhat dazed and concussed and spent the rest of the afternoon lying in a shallow slit trench not really worrying what was going on around me. One thing I do remember was a bombardier from a Bofors light AA gun that was about a hundred yards away walking across to me with his water bottle and offering me a drink. Considering that water was worth its weight in gold, that the ground he had walked across had until recently been smothered in bursting shells, and could be again at any moment, it was a very charitable thing to do. I do not remember if it was the same day but once, during a similar lull, the gunners of the HAC (Honourable Artillery Company) left their gun pits and 25-pounders and were playing football in the heat of the day just behind their guns – I don't know where they got their energy from.

The platoon commander decided I should go back to B Echelon that night – I think perhaps because I was still a bit light-headed rather than because of the difficulty I would have with a large field dressing on my hand. It took nearly all night to get back to B Echelon and next day we were bombed four times, just to show that it was not going to be all peace and quiet. There I had the first glimpse of the gulf that separated the troops who spent their time up the 'sharp end' and those who lived behind the lines. I might have expected this further back towards base, but hardly within my own company. I reported to our colour sergeant to ask about rations, since I had to eat somewhere (to sleep all I needed was a patch of desert and there was plenty of that). I expected him to tell me to muck in with his crew of drivers, storemen, etc. There were at least a dozen of them and they lived well on buckshee rations. Instead he said, 'You don't expect me to issue rations for one man do you? You'd better report to HQ Company and get rations from them.' Knowing that I would only get a similar (but even more blunt) answer from them I was thinking I had better get back to the company as soon as I had had my hand dressed when I came across one of the gun crews from our company. They were there having their truck repaired and they took me in and shared their rations with me. After a few days my hand was better and I was ready to go back, and then I had a chance to get my own back. The trucks were all lined up ready to start – I was sitting in the back of the ration truck – when German heavy guns dropped a few shells about a mile away. I was just passing some comment about them when I became conscious of the fact that I was alone. Looking round I spotted a few tin hats sticking out of slit trenches about a hundred yards away. The shelling soon stopped, but it seemed clear that none of them were going to emerge until they had to so I started looking round the truck. The rations had already been put into separate sacks for each platoon, so as to minimise the time spent up the sharp end. It was not unknown for the colour sergeant to hurl the sacks out of the moving truck, shouting 'Captain X says we mustn't stop – got to go straight back.' Further exploration at the back of the truck revealed their own private store of rations, which was considerable, so I rapidly transferred a few tins of the more desirable items – milk, fruit, sausages etc. – into my own platoon's sack. We set off after dark but couldn't find the company and had to wait until daylight. We eventually met them just as they were about to beat a rapid retreat under very heavy shellfire, much to the horror of the B Echelon people. In the chaos I somehow found myself helping one of the other crews to get their gun out, but I eventually found my way back to my own section and my diary notes: 'Glad to be back.'

We were in the same old area in the Cauldron, between El Adem and Knightsbridge, shelling and being shelled – chased out one day and moving back the next. Four days later our new 6-pounder guns arrived and we had to make a swift transfer, pulling the old guns out of the gun pits and putting the new ones in. We were glad to have something that might be able to do some damage to Jerry, although it was not so handy to manoeuvre. Two days later we had a very sticky time which proved to be the beginning of the end of the Gazala Line battle. It started when our brigade was temporarily put under command of the 7th Armoured Division, whose commander (he who had already been taken prisoner once) decided to go off and have an argument with the corps commander. On the way he ran into some Jerries and had to hide in a well for the rest of the day. Meanwhile our brigade was still sitting waiting for some orders from him when we were suddenly attacked from the rear by the 21st Panzer Division. Our tanks hopped it and we had a difficult time getting our guns out of action under some very accurate fire. We moved back a couple of miles but were still being attacked on three sides by tanks and lorried infantry and by nightfall they were partway round the fourth side, the 4th Armoured Brigade on our left having been chased halfway back to Tobruk. We managed to get out after dark even though our portee had a 50 mm shot which passed through the ration box and top of the bonnet, taking a piece of the steering wheel on the way out through the back. Luckily the driver was not in his seat at the time. Two of the other three portees were also damaged but not put out of action, though one of them had a 50 mm shot rattling around in its front differential. Next day we tried to help the Guards withstand heavy attacks on their box, but by evening our three armoured brigades had lost 105 tanks in two days and had only 50 left between them. The following morning about twenty German tanks arrived with breakfast, but instead of coming close enough for us to open up, they sat back and engaged us with HE (High Explosive rounds) and machine guns and we had another very sticky withdrawal. One of our portees had a direct hit, but they managed to tow the gun away with the three-tonner. We moved north to the minefield running north from Acroma where we had to make a 'last stand' because beyond the minefield and below the escarpment was the coast road, along which the 1st South African Division were streaming. They had been ordered, much to their disgust as they had hardly been engaged during the past three weeks, to evacuate the Gazala position and withdraw through Tobruk to the Egyptian frontier, and they needed the rest of the day and the night to get clear.

June 1942

I'm writing a few lines while I've got the chance, as Rommel seems to be doing his best to interrupt our letter writing activities these days, as well as putting the kybosh on my leave for the time being. I shall feel very strange when I do eventually get back to civilisation. You can't imagine what it feels like, not seeing any streets, shops, houses or civilians for over six months. Nothing but sand and rocks, though I have seen one tree!

Our platoon was very lucky here because the German attack just missed us and fell on the rest of the company. Half of 6 and the whole of 7 and 8 Platoons, having first knocked out a few German tanks, were overrun and lost all ten guns. A handful of the 60-70 in the crews got away on two portees, but the rest were missing – most of them captured. That night we were able to start getting away, but there was a problem. As well as having to 'gap' the minefield behind us, the escarpment was negotiable for vehicles only in one or two places. Eventually a way was found and by morning we had made our way down to the road where we joined a nose-to-tail procession with the South Africans. Luckily we were only bombed once and only a few shells came over. We left Tobruk through a gap in the perimeter minefield southeast towards Sidi Rezegh. For some reason I was travelling in the front beside the driver when halfway through the minefield there was a big bang and I went sailing up in the air. I thought at first it was a shell but when the smoke cleared I realised we had hit a mine with the front nearside wheel – luckily the mine was one of ours (probably made in Egypt) and not a German one, or I would have been somewhat damaged since I was only just above and behind the wheel. There was a roll of bedding on the floor which helped to absorb the shock. One of the South Africans nearby laughed and said, 'You're the third to do that this morning' and I realised that a Honey tank had gone slightly off the track, carried away the barbed wire fence marking the safe line and then blown its track off. In the dust cloud thrown up by the vehicles in front of us we had unwittingly followed the displaced barbed wire and blown ourselves up. The South Africans seemed to have been content to have watched all this without making any attempt to repair the wire. We got the gun off the portee, hitched it onto the platoon truck, transferred our kit and carried on out to the Ed Duda escarpment. For the first day for three weeks there was no shelling. We started back that night, moving via Gambut, Bir Sheferzen and Sofafi to find ourselves three days later, on 18 June, on the beach between Buq Buq and Sidi Barrani. We just had time for a swim before eleven new 6-pounders arrived to replace the ones we had lost, bringing us up to sixteen again, but to find the crews was more difficult. Only Sam the driver and I remained on our crew, the rest being split amongst the other guns. The new No. 1 was a lance corporal who had been with the 2nd Battalion (he was a golf professional in civvy street) and we had one other chap who had had anti-tank training. The fifth man was an old soldier – a regular reservist who had been in the QM stores; there was no sixth man. We had three days in which to sort ourselves out and test the gun. Whilst doing this we were filmed by a cameraman who made us put our thumbs up after we had fired. He then went and poured a can of petrol over a derelict German tank and filmed it burning!

Whilst there we heard the news that Tobruk had fallen, a shock at the time but it later became clear that it was inevitable. When the Gazala Line was established at the beginning of the year it had been decided that if we were forced back, no attempt would be made to hold Tobruk, not least because the Navy were unwilling to accept a repetition of the casualties they had suffered in keeping it supplied the previous time. London was informed accordingly and the defences were allowed to deteriorate. Mines had been lifted for use in the Gazala Line, barbed wire had been flattened and the anti-tank ditch partly filled in with sand. But when we started pulling back from Gazala, Churchill stuck his oar in and said that on no account was Tobruk to be given up. However, there was no time to organise the defences as Rommel moved in straight away, using the plan he had prepared the previous November. Although the South Africans got a lot of the blame because they formed a large part of the garrison, the break-in actually took place through an Indian brigade. A series of Stuka raids on the minefields detonated the mines, so the tanks were able to go straight over the filled-in anti-tank ditch, through the minefield and into the heart of the perimeter. Once they had started swarming around there, the rest of the garrison had no hope of holding out.

On 22 June we moved off to join the 22nd Armoured Brigade, with whom we were destined to spend the rest of the war. They had only one composite regiment of tanks at that time. Whilst our own 2nd Armoured Brigade went back to the Delta to reorganise, we moved via Sidi Barrani, Misheifa and Charing Cross to a landing ground – LG75 – which we covered for 24 hours whilst the RAF got their aircraft and equipment away. We then set off east another 70 miles to join the brigade near Minqar Qaim, having collected six days rations as it was unlikely that the Echelons would be able to reach us. We were bombed for the second night running but unfortunately this time it was by the RAF and not the Luftwaffe. They were at it for four hours and two of our chaps were wounded, one of them losing a leg. The only consolation was that the Luftwaffe was doing the same thing to Jerry columns not far north of us.

We spent a couple of days looking for Jerry and wondering what he was up to, but on the morning of the 27th he appeared with a vengeance. As we carried out a 'crash' ground action, a shell burst right alongside the portee and our ex-regular ex-QM storeman went off his

*Crew of a German armoured personnel carrier; "Knightsbridge", June 1942
(captured German film)*

head and started running round in circles screaming. This was the only experience I had throughout the war of anyone really going crackers (there were a couple of occasions when I had a job to persuade someone to get out of his slit trench, but that was all). This made things a little difficult as we were trying to get the gun into action and the air was full of shot and shell, so somebody clocked him one and we dumped him on the portee when it went off. I never saw him again. This left only three of us, apart from the driver, to handle the gun, which was hard going. The 21st Panzer eventually gave up shelling us and moved on eastwards leaving us behind. We moved back another 50 miles that night, at the end of which we found that the other three guns of our platoon were missing – someone had fallen asleep during one of the halts and not noticed that the column had moved on. It was several days before they rejoined. In the meantime we attached ourselves to 8 Platoon and joined a column made up of our A Company and a battery of guns plus a composite squadron of Honey tanks. These were quite good and reliable American-made light tanks but their popgun made them no match for the German tanks. We went out looking for the Afrika Korps and eventually found it. Despite my protests I was ordered by some twit of an officer from A Company to open fire on a German tank that was miles out of range. Even firing at maximum elevation my shots were hitting the ground well in front of him and I don't think he realised we were firing at him. We couldn't get any nearer because there was a minefield in the way, although we suspected it was only a dummy but couldn't be sure.

That night in leaguer we heard a rumbling of tanks and stood-to hastily. It proved to be the 15th Panzer Division moving forward by night; they were less than a quarter of a mile away and seemed to take hours to pass but we kept quiet as mice and they didn't spot us. Next day, 30 June, was one of the most enjoyable I spent in the desert. Following on behind the 15th Panzer we picked up all their crocks. We knocked out two tanks that had broken down (they don't really count) and four trucks and also chased off an 88 mm gun that started shelling us. But best of all was the stuff we recovered that the Germans had got hold of in Tobruk – a case of milk, tins of cheese and fruit, cigarettes etc. which set us up for quite a while. Then we bumped into another of our columns, which included a company from our 2nd Battalion, and together we caught up with the rear of the 15th Panzer, captured some more 3-tonners and prisoners, and one of our guns knocked out a tank.

By nightfall we still had 50 miles to go to reach the Alamein position, with the Afrika Korps in-between, so we set off in the dark, driving through several German and Italian leaguers – they were too surprised to open up on us until it was too late – and picking up a few more prisoners on the way. By dawn we still had twelve miles to go, with German columns on both sides of us. Two of our portees got stuck in soft sand and had to be burned and the Honey tanks were so short of petrol that half of them were towing the other half. Then one of them was knocked out by a captured 6-pounder that the Germans were using, so we went out and exchanged shots with it – a fairly fruitless pastime since it was very difficult to damage one another with solid shot – but it kept him occupied. As we approached Alamein the South Africans started shelling us – they were not to know that the centre of the three columns approaching them was British. As we passed through their lines, two of the Springboks gave us a carton of 4,000 cigarettes.

The Desert – At Alamein

The next month was pretty hectic. Both armies had been slogging away for a month and had suffered considerable losses; the troops were very tired. It was like two punch-drunk boxers still slogging it out in the fifteenth round. Our two armoured brigades had about 100 tanks between them, equal to two weak regiments compared with the nine we had a month before, and only a third were Grants with their heavy guns. On 2 July we moved straight on to the Ruweisat Ridge and dug in but because of the shortage of tanks they decided to use us as 'armour'. With the guns up 'on portee' we reversed into action alongside the tanks. We had to reverse because the gun fired over the back of the truck. Because there was a lot of soft sand in the area south of Ruweisat where we were operating, we had Honey tanks standing by to tow us out if we got stuck and Crusaders to bring us up ammunition and petrol. We put in an attack in the afternoon and met the 21st Panzer Division head on as it advanced to attack us. We fired over 100 rounds with our gun (we had to pull back for more after we had used the 70 we carried) and it got pretty hot. I don't know that we did a comparable amount of damage – we claimed five tanks between us – but we must have given them a few frights with the high velocity shots whistling past their ears. We weren't very anxious to close the range too much, being stuck up on the portee with machine-gun as well as shell fire to cope with. That night in the leaguer the tank crews said they were 'very glad to have us with them', which we thought a bit rich considering they were sitting behind several inches of armour. On the other hand, a solid shot that would devastate them if it penetrated their armour would just whistle through or past our portee without a great deal of risk. Next morning, 3 July, we repeated the process, but our platoon did not get a shoot, just got shot at. Unluckily, just as we were moving into leaguer a stray shell, the last of the day, killed one of our chaps and took the arm off another. It was one of the ironies that we could go through two days under direct fire almost the whole of the time and then get caught by a random shell. We got our own back next morning, however, as we opened out from leaguer on Ruweisat Ridge at dawn. We peeped over the ridge and found a big column of tanks and trucks leaguered in the wadi below. We blazed away with everything and hit a number of tanks before the survivors withdrew in disorder – even our Bren gunner was able to get off over 1,000 rounds. We had one or two casualties from small arms fire and one of my old friends Dicky Dyer was hit by shrapnel (he recovered but was later killed at Caen). In the afternoon we pushed along the ridge and our guns knocked out two more German tanks. Rommel was forced to give up for the time being and the regimental history says 'It was the 1st Battalion … who played as large a part as any one unit in halting the Afrika Korps.' [1]

At Alamein after a wash! – July 1942

We then moved back for a couple of days rest and maintenance, then forwards again south of Ruweisat for the next two weeks. One or two of our guns had a shoot, mainly at long range. About this time, due to the shortage of people who could read and write and follow a map, I was appointed lance corporal (temporary unpaid).

On 22 July the New Zealanders put in an attack and our tanks were supposed to support them at first light but were slow to arrive, and the New Zealanders were overrun by German tanks. A New Zealand colonel came rushing up to us and demanded that we open fire on some German tanks. We pointed out that they were too far away for us to do any damage but he insisted, so we had a

---

[1]   Hastings, R.H.W.S., *The Rifle Brigade in the Second World War 1939–1945*, Page 137.

crack. I hit two of them but doubt if the shots penetrated at that range. This attracted a lot of shellfire in our direction, in the middle of which we were bombed by a mixed force of Stukas and Ju 88's which caused us some casualties. These included one of our corporals who was killed standing up firing a Bren at them, which was a foolish thing to do. We were glad when things quietened down a bit. A week later we moved back a couple of miles and I noted in my diary, 'Saw no shells today – the first day for a long time.' Three days later we moved back twelve miles into Corps Reserve. We were always glad of the opportunity of completely unloading the portee and our kit, clearing out all the sand, tidying everything up and putting it back again in the right places. It often seemed to happen that if we were told we would be stopping for 24 hours, we would get everything off, only to be told to be ready to move in an hour. On other occasions we would be at an hour's notice and stay for a week.

Three events were now looming up: we were due to go back to the Delta for rest and refit, my leave was getting nearer and Rommel was expected to have a final push at getting to the Delta. The question was in which order these events would occur. In the end the first never took place (our 9th Battalion, which was due to relieve us, had to be disbanded in order to provide reinforcements for the other three battalions of the regiment in the desert). I just managed to get my leave in before Rommel made his move but not soon enough to celebrate my 21st birthday in comfort. Meanwhile we were engaged on various exercises in preparation for the expected attack, occupying alternative positions according to which way Rommel might move. One of them was the Alam Halfa Ridge where we dug our gun pits. Montgomery, who had not then arrived in the desert, later claimed to have spotted that this was the vital defence position.

Back here in the Alamein position we found the desert much more crowded than we had been used to. With a comparatively narrow front and Alex only 60 miles away, most of the desert seemed to be occupied by vehicles of some sort whereas up in the wide-open spaces of Libya one could go for miles without seeing another unit. It is one of the curiosities of the army that it seems to take a hundred men at the rear to keep one soldier at the front. Moving up from the rear, one passed through a mass of camps – supply depots, ordinance workshops, pioneer units, tank delivery squadrons, sub-area HQs, provost companies and heaven knows what. Then, at varying distances depending on how far forward the front was, there would be Army HQ, Corps HQ, corps and divisional supply columns and transport units, then Main Div. HQ, the B Echelons and Main Brigade HQ. Then the country started to look relatively uninhabited as one reached the business end. The battalions, batteries and tank regiments are usually fairly widely scattered and as unobtrusive as possible, with vehicles well dispersed.

At Alamein we could not disperse as much as we would have liked, but the RAF were keeping the Luftwaffe away and when they did appear they had such a wide range of targets that one was unlucky to cop it, although we did once or twice. With so many troops around, the flies were a bigger menace than ever and almost drove us mad, and the constant movement of vehicles in areas where there was already a lot of soft sand caused that to blow around continuously. On the other hand, the proximity to the Delta made the supply position much easier. Water was relatively plentiful and rations were better (even oranges, water melons and dried apple rings) and as we had flour, those with culinary pretensions were able to try their hand at duffs, cakes, etc. Cigarettes and other NAAFI supplies were more plentiful and we even got some cans of beer. These were treated with great suspicion as we had never seen them before (they tended to get very gassy in the heat). Luckily there were a handful of Americans attached to our tank regiments to get battle experience who had some bottled beer which they happily exchanged for our cans. We used to bury bottles in the sand early in morning to keep them cool until we wanted them and occasionally enjoyed watching the frantic digging of someone who had forgotten just where he'd buried his bottle. We also got some 'comforts'. The 'Kumangetit Fund' (I can't remember who they were) presented us with two eggs each, as well as Worcestershire Sauce, lime juice and cake, and we were also given a pair of army boots and small pillows by 'the ladies of Alexandria' which were very comfortable to rest one's head on. Periodically I used to get a large fruit cake from a friend of the family in New Zealand which always went down very well with the troops.

August 1942

As you will have seen in the papers, things have quietened down a bit now, and we are taking it easy. I'm hoping to get my long-lost leave before very long. I hoped it would be in time for my birthday but no such luck. I haven't even got the 'key of the door' now – I've lost that somewhere in the desert! (I hope someone's in when I get home!)

On 13 August I celebrated my 21st birthday with PT, maintenance, a brigade exercise with the tanks and a headache and temperature. My leave was due in a week and, as Rommel didn't interfere, I went back to B Echelon on the 19th and by midday next day we were in Alex. My companion was 'Lefty' Wright, who had been with the platoon from Farnham days and was an insurance agent in civil life. We first went to Mustapha Barracks to make contact with another ex-member of our platoon, 'Jacko' Jackson, who had been taken ill when we first arrived in Egypt and had a cushy job in the barracks. He was very conscience-stricken about this and we had to keep encouraging him to accept his good fortune and not take active steps to get back to the battalion. We spent the next four days looking round the shops and bazaar, dodging the beggars and shoe-shine boys and swimming during the day. In the evenings we went to the pictures twice, but the first time there was an air raid warning so we went back to bed and the second time I slept through the film. We had some good meals in restaurants (chicken and chips and fruit salad and ice cream were a favourite) and it seemed strange to sit at a table and be waited on. We found it fascinating to turn on a tap and just let the water flow and walking on level pavements was also an experience. The bath I had was, except for a few dips in the Med, the first since we were in Cape Town over nine months previously.

August 1942

Well, I'm on leave at last, we arrived (that is, Lefty Wright and I) at midday the day before yesterday (20th) and have to go back on the morning of the 25th. We were rather disappointed at having to go to Alex instead of Cairo, as we'd already seen Alex, but we are enjoying ourselves nevertheless, especially as we've met Jackson who used to be in our platoon, and is now stationed here; he knows the ropes and is able to show us around.

We are staying at the YMCA and couldn't do better. For 3 shillings a night we get bed (real sheets and a spring mattress you sink right through), early morning tea, a good breakfast, and showers etc. It took us the first day to get rid of the dirt of nine months, but after a shave, shower, haircut and shampoo, we felt a bit better and proceeded to get down to the business of eating.

All we do is eat, sleep, drink, see a few shows and stroll around, but it's wonderful what a change it makes. The last time I slept in a 'civvy' bed was August 18th last year.

Official portrait – Alexandria, August 1942

We set off back on the morning of the 25th, reaching the company at Alam Halfa next morning, where we found them still waiting on the top line for Rommel's push. This finally came on 31 August, when he advanced through the minefields at the southern end, delayed by our 2nd and 7th battalions in the 7th Motor Brigade. Looking south from our positions we watched the 4th Light Armoured Brigade withdrawing eastwards, firing over the back of their tanks as they went, with the Afrika Korps following. When they came level with us our tanks were ordered to 'show themselves', so they moved forward and fired a few shots where-upon the German tanks turned and headed for us on the forward slopes of the Alam Halfa Ridge. This was a crucial battle because it was Rommel's last chance to reach the Delta and our brigade – known as the ELH Brigade (Egypt's Last Hope) because it contained nearly all our remaining tanks – was the force mainly relied upon to stop him. We were dug in on the forward slope with a squadron of Grants of the CLY (County of London Yeomanry) behind us. As the German tanks – about 80 of them – approached, their artillery opened up a heavy barrage on our positions and the Stukas made a rare appearance but concentrated on the gun and transport lines behind us. When they had got to within about 1,000 yards, both sides opened up and within a few minutes very nearly all the CLY's Grants had been knocked out, a number of them in flames. The damage was done mainly by a new German tank – the Mark IV Special – which had a new long-barrelled 75 mm gun that was able to penetrate the frontal armour of the Grants. Luckily the Grant nearest to us, about ten yards away, although hit with two of the crew killed, did not blow up or we would have had a very warm time.

We did not get a chance to fire a shot from our gun as nothing came within our arc of fire and we were defiladed from the front by a bit of a bump in the ground (that is, there was a slight rise in the ground in front of us and we were aiming to a flank). I would have been less scared if I had been busy firing back than just lying there with the earth erupting all around. The company was said to have knocked out nineteen tanks in all, including five credited to an old friend of mine from Farnham days, Lance Sergeant Norman Griffiths. He was awarded the DCM and was later commissioned and returned to the company as an officer at Homs. Two of our platoons, 7 and 8, were overrun and two chaps were killed when a grenade was thrown from a tank into their gun pit and another was killed whilst getting away on a truck. Most crews were told to start walking towards the German positions but their infantry were not following up closely and when our chaps had gone a short way most of them dived into convenient slit trenches and made their way back to us after dark. I think we had eleven missing in the end. We were able to recover the guns during the night. One of the chaps was crouching in his slit trench when a German tank stopped right beside him, and the tank commander tapped his wrist and shouted '*Uhr*'. The chap replied 'Half past six' whereupon the Jerry showed every sign of rage and shouted '*Nein, nein, geben Sie mir*' so he reluctantly surrendered his watch. For some reason the first thing anyone did with a prisoner, on both sides, was to pinch his watch, almost before he had been disarmed. There must have been a great shortage of watches in POW camps.

The German tanks were gradually edging closer from a direction in which we could not fire at them. I was anxiously calculating how long it would take for the sun to go down, and how near the tanks would be by then, when there was a rumble and over the ridge behind us roared the Grant squadrons of the Royal Scots Greys, the brigade's reserve armoured regiment. Apparently they had been a bit slow moving and the brigadier, 'Pip' Roberts, had urged them over the air, 'Come on the Greys, get the whip out.' Anyway, it was a marvellous sight to see 30 Grants come roaring down and open fire simultaneously. One of them stopped only a few yards behind our gun pit and the blast deafened us. When we made our presence known the tank commander said, 'Good God, I didn't know anyone was still alive down there.' The arrival of the Greys was too much for the Germans, who had already suffered considerable losses from the CLY and from our own guns, so they decided they had had enough for one day and pulled back. As dusk fell it was a relief to be able to stand up and stretch our legs again. We found there were still two chaps in the Grant knocked out near our pit; one was dead and the other dying and it was a difficult job getting them out, especially until the MO turned up with morphia. We then had a somewhat nervous night, fearing that the Germans might send their infantry in to knock out the anti-tank guns, and as we had no infantry with us it was somewhat lonely with no one else around except another of our guns about 200 yards away. In the end all was quiet except for the RAF busily bombing the German leaguers. The following day Jerry made a half-hearted attack to the left of us but got nowhere. For the next two days there was a lot of artillery activity and plenty of bombing. We used to take great delight in watching the

6-pounder in recoil

Bostons dropping their loads on the Afrika Korps with great regularity (ten times in a day) – the Imperturbable Eighteen we used to call them. Our night bombers were also very active. The Luftwaffe were also over, but the RAF got amongst them and we saw a number of Ju 88's and Stukas brought down. By then Rommel had decided he had had enough; he had lost nearly half his tanks and was very short of petrol, so he started pulling back again to the minefield.

In the regimental history reference is made to the Alam Halfa action 'This brought them [the German tanks] right on top of the 6-pounder guns of B Company ... they reacted magnificently: they held their fire to within three hundred yards, and Sergeant Griffiths's gun knocked out five tanks. It is said that nineteen enemy tanks were destroyed by these guns alone. Although one platoon was overrun, this action had a decisive effect on the battle.'[2]

August 1942

I'm glad to see that at last people are realising that it is impossible to keep on producing weapons inferior to those of the enemy, though of course things have been different since the 'General Grants' came out here. It seems to be Britain all over – 'muddling through' as usual. Thank God for the Russians anyway, I hope they hang on in the Caucasus till winter ...

I see Brazil is now at war. It is slowly spreading; it's a real world war this time and no mistake. I only wish it would shorten it a bit.

---

[2]   Hastings, R.H.W.S., *The Rifle Brigade in the Second World War 1939–1945.* Page 147.

We stayed where we were for a week, resting and doing maintenance. The 22nd Armoured Brigade, which had been under command of the 10th Armoured Division for the Alam Halfa battle now returned, permanently as it transpired, to the 7th Armoured Division. They had told us in August that they were going to reorganise the battalion again. Instead of three motor companies each of two motor platoons, one carrier platoon and one machine gun platoon (which had replaced the third motor platoon in the spring), plus one anti-tank company of four platoons, we were to have four motor companies again, each of which comprised one motor platoon, one carrier platoon, one machine gun platoon and one anti-tank platoon. So B Company became a motor company again and 5 Platoon a carrier platoon once more. Our 9th Battalion had been disbanded earlier in August, as they were unable to get sufficient reinforcements to maintain four battalions of the Rifle Brigade in the desert, so we had received a large draft from them to bring us up to strength again.

I was in a carrier with a sergeant from the 9th Battalion and a driver who had been in the 2nd, but for some time the crews seemed to be changing round every few days. They did not waste any time on letting us get used to our new role, or to one another. We got the carriers one day, and the next we moved forward to our minefields, which were called Nuts and May (Jerry had two on his side which were called January and February). The whole area became a maze of minefields which the Germans called, very appropriately, *Teufelsgarten* (Devil's Garden). The next two weeks we spent protecting the minefields at night against Jerry patrols, lifting parties etc. (they never did come) and resting and doing maintenance during the day. Then we moved a bit farther south and spent another fortnight going out beyond our minefields every night to cover a working party of sappers who were digging mysterious holes. I never did find out what they were for but I suspect it was all part of the deception plan to make Rommel believe our attack was coming in the south. We spent the days resting, but there were frequent sandstorms and we also had a lot of attention from Messerschmitt fighter-bombers.

After that we pulled out for two days rest on the coast which included 24 hours leave in Alex. Apart from eating, we went to the pictures (*Dr Jekyll and Mr Hyde*) and spent the night at the Red Shield (Salvation Army). On the way back to our positions in the south of the line our carrier broke down and had to be towed into workshops. The carriers we had been given when we handed over our anti-tank guns were a ropey collection, always giving trouble and not what we would have wished for going into a major battle, unlike the ones we had originally brought out with us from England. While it was being repaired I took charge of the platoon truck whilst one of the chaps was on leave. This was probably lucky for me as we were coming up to the big Alamein attack, which started on 23 October. Although they did not tell us at the time, the main attack was to be made up north near the coast and our attack in the south was only a diversion to keep the 21st Panzer Division occupied. The 1st and 10th Armoured Divisions had been completely re-equipped with Sherman tanks, self-propelled field guns etc., and were to form a Corps de Chasse which would break out and chase the Afrika Korps out of Libya. The 7th Armoured, however, was given no new equipment – our armoured regiments had only Grants and Crusaders (with fewer Grants than the others had Shermans) and our carriers were barely battle-worthy. Whereas in the north the break-in was to be made by the infantry divisions, in the south we had to make our own and we were told that this was our job. In the words of our brigadier 'If they ask us to go beyond Matruh, we shall have to walk because none of the vehicles will make it.' In the event things didn't work out like that. We were feeling fairly confident of the outcome of the battle, not because of the presence of Montgomery but because we had six fully equipped armoured brigades (twice as many as we'd ever had before), all the new tanks and other equipment, two new infantry divisions from England (the Home Counties and the Highland) and complete superiority in the air.

The gaps in the minefields were to be made by the sappers, covered by the carriers of the 44th Recce Regiment, with the new Scorpion flail tanks to help them lift the mines. Our company was to go through the two left-hand gaps and A Company the two on the right, to form a bridgehead on the far side through which the armour could advance;

the rest of the brigade would follow. Having dealt with the first minefield (January) in this way, the second (February) would be similarly penetrated. I cannot believe this was the best way to do it. The whole brigade's vehicles were lined up nose to tail in four columns stretching from the German minefield back across no-man's land through the gaps in our own minefield and beyond. It has been described as being like 'Epsom High Street on Derby day' and 'the car park at Cheltenham Races'. They used the same method in the attack in the north. The troops facing us were an Italian parachute division, the Folgore, a fairly tough lot. As soon as they realised where the gaps were being made, their guns, machine guns and mortars opened up. Some vehicles were set on fire, lighting the scene up like daylight and making it even easier for them. Our company had a difficult time getting through and when they finally emerged from January they had to knock out a number of machine gun nests and anti-tank guns. They had quite a lot of casualties with the company commander and two other officers wounded, and two of the sergeants in our platoon killed – Mac Mulford and Graham Bradbury. Both were regulars and both had been awarded the Military Medal only shortly before. They were first-class types who instilled great confidence in those serving under them and we were all very depressed that they had gone.

In the meantime I was stuck in the queue in my three-tonner in the old no-man's land between the British and German minefields with only the occasional shell coming my way. Next day my carrier came back from workshops, so I was able to go up to rejoin B Company which by then had been combined with A Company, as they had both suffered so many casualties including both company commanders. The second-in-command of the battalion took command temporarily. It had not been possible to gap the second minefield, February, during the first night, and it was impossible during the day because the Italians were sitting on Himeimat, a hill to the south of us which gave them a clear view over the whole of the battlefield (the Free French had tried to push them off but failed). So on the second night the Queens went through us to force a gap in the second field. This they did, but when a squadron of the CLY went through, each tank was knocked out in turn as it emerged on the far side of the gap. As the division was under orders not to lose too many tanks in case they were needed at a later stage (how right they were), the attack was not pressed and on the third night we left the front to the Queens and pulled back to the old no-man's land. The battalion had suffered pretty badly – nineteen officers had been killed or wounded, almost two out of three. The final blow for our platoon happened to another of my old friends, Pat Sydes. He was accidentally shot when an Italian automatic rifle he had picked up went off, apparently when his carrier hit a bump, and he died on the way to hospital. After coming safely through those three days it was a tragic way to go. By now we were very short of crews – we almost had a carrier each. I had to take one back to workshops for repairs. Soon after my return we moved up north, behind the front where the real breakthrough was not going according to Monty's plan. The infantry had not got as far as expected and not enough time had been allowed for mine-clearing so he had sent the armour in before the breakthrough had been made and they had suffered heavy losses (we lost about 500 tanks altogether during the battle). Our 2nd Battalion had a bad time here. They went forward and occupied a feature called Kidney Ridge, the expected support did not come up, and they held out against continuous tank attacks all day, knocking out 32 tanks. Their colonel, Vic Turner who had previously been second-in-command, was awarded the VC.

October 1942

I'm sorry I haven't written before but as you will guess from the papers we are once more having a busy time and there is little opportunity for writing, nor do the officers have much time for censoring letters.

By the way, Capt. Jepson Turner has just been awarded the MC, you remember his brother got the DSO.

Out here things are bound to progress slowly at first owing to the confined space in which to manoeuvre, but we are all very confident as to the ultimate result. The Air Force, as usual, are working wonders. One can hardly ever see the Luftwaffe these days, and even then only in ones and twos.

We waited at Tel El Eisa whilst the final gaps were made and went through the minefield in the usual nose-to-tail queue in the afternoon of the 3rd and into the night. On the way, one of our sergeants was killed by one of our own shells falling short – sad, but it happened from time to time. At last we got through into the open and after a few miles got involved in a tank battle with the Italians. No longer being on anti-tank guns, we couldn't take part in it but we got very heavily shelled and lost a couple more wounded.

The Desert – Pursuit to Tunis

୧୬ᘐ୨

Next day the chase was on and we covered over 60 miles, finishing up south of Fuka, picking up many prisoners on the way. The following morning we set off again, heading north-west towards the coast. After twenty miles we bumped into the Afrika Korps rearguard, but our tanks ran out of petrol and we had to let them get away. As the division had not been originally intended to take part in the pursuit, it had been allotted no extra transport for increased petrol requirements whilst by all accounts there were still colossal traffic jams through the gaps in the Alamein minefields (the official history says that traffic control and driving discipline were outstandingly bad). As the tanks took about three gallons to the mile, and even our carriers only did about three miles to the gallon, petrol was a major factor. It started to rain as we went into leaguer for the night; eventually we had to give up trying to sleep as we were lying in pools of water, so we just huddled in the carrier with a groundsheet over our heads. We spent the next morning towing out trucks that were stuck in the mud. Then we had to transfer temporarily to I Company as they had lost all their carriers. We started off westward again, going ahead of the column and picking up more stragglers, but eventually a bogie gave way and we had to stop and repair it. It was dark by the time we caught up with the column again south of Minqar Qaim and found one of our other carriers had fallen down a steep bank and lost both its tracks, which gave them a tricky repair job. Here we were inflicted with a brand-new subaltern who had come from base to join I Company and took over our carrier. The first morning he got out a large washbasin and started pouring most of the contents of a can of water into it. I asked him what he thought he was doing and he said he was going to have a wash. I said

'Not with that water; that is the whole day's ration for all of us – pour it back and if you spill a drop you get no tea today.' He reluctantly complied and stayed dirty. Just after we started off another bogie went so we had a 60 mile chase after the column; the morning after, we managed 24 miles before a third bogie went, with another 60 miles before we were able to catch up. The armoured cars of the 'Cherry Pickers', the 11th Hussars, had crossed the wire into Libya and we followed them at first light next morning, the first of the army back into Libya. The 7th Armoured was the only armoured division to continue the pursuit into Libya, although as the divisional history says: 'Unlike the other two armoured divisions, the 7th had not been re-equipped with new tanks and their old ones had for the most part exceeded by far their theoretical mileage … In consequence many of the tanks of the 22nd Brigade which had taken part in the Knightsbridge battles had travelled many miles in the desert already.'[3]

We were about 40 miles south of the coast and we immediately turned north towards Capuzzo with the object of cutting off the Afrika Korps rearguard before it got up the pass at Sollum, but again we were held up by lack of petrol and it was not until the next day that we got going again and engaged his rearguard at Capuzzo, too late to cut him off. An engine and one truck went racing off along the railway towards Tobruk, fired at and missed by every tank in sight. This was the third chance that had been missed and Rommel was able to get the remnants of his troops safely away to El Agheila. Montgomery has been blamed because he confined himself to making short jabs up to the coast, whereas the armoured divisional commanders recommended one division should be given sufficient transport and supplies to take a wider sweep further south (where the going was better and we would not have been bogged down by rain) and to emerge on the coast road much further west before the Afrika Korps had got back that far, but Monty would not take that risk.

---

3   Verney, G.L., *The Desert Rats: The History of the 7th Armoured Division 1939 to 1945.* Page 136.

From Capuzzo our combined A/B Company went in to occupy Bardia with the 11th Hussars, but we were still with I Company and we moved west to occupy the Sidi Azeiz airfield and then moved on to El Adem, south of Tobruk, where we stopped to sort ourselves out. A, B and I Companies had between them only eight carriers out of 30, three anti-tank guns out of twelve, two Vickers machine guns out of twelve and not many 15-cwt motor sections. Nor were there many tanks remaining in the armoured regiments. It was decided to send the armoured cars across the desert to Msus and then to Benghazi, and A/B Company went with them. We tried to get back to them, but the carriers were too worn out and only wheeled vehicles were taken. We were left with I Company and within three days they had us on drill parade and PT and all the carriers were sent into the workshops for new engines. When they came back they were to be handed over to I Company. Then we moved up to El Mrassas, west of Tobruk. By now I was not feeling well, being sick after every meal, especially fried bully, and feeling feverish. I had thought at first it was just nerves and put up with it whilst we were on the chase, but after a week of PT etc. I decided to report sick.

The MO told me I had jaundice and would be due for a 'nice rest'. I was sent back via the Advanced Dressing Station to the Casualty Clearing Station (CCS) where I spent two nights before being flown back from El Adem in a Lodestar (the transport version of a Lockheed Hudson), my first flight. I thought I must be pretty bad if they sent me back by air, but in fact they were using the aircraft to bring petrol and supplies up and they would otherwise have gone back empty. There were no seats – we all just sat on the floor but we had to pack up to the front of the plane for take-off which made us a bit nervous. It was curious flying back over the desert and the old battlefields and seeing how the slit trenches, vehicle tracks etc. looked from the air. At the CCS they had only two forms of diet – liquids and solids. I was on liquids which meant tea and soup. By now I was feeling better and by the time I got on the plane I was feeling hungry. So I occupied the time by eating my emergency ration – a thick block of enriched chocolate supposed to keep one going for, I think, 48 hours. We landed at

THE DESERT – PURSUIT TO TUNIS

Heliopolis, outside Cairo, and went to No. 9 General Hospital in the old Heliopolis Palace Hotel. I was taken to a ward where the sister promptly held her fingers to her nose and said, 'Take those filthy rags off and get into the bath' and I realised what a scarecrow I must have looked. After being seen by a doctor the sister told me I could get up, but 'not to go down to the canteen stuffing yourself with cream buns.' I asked her how long I was likely to be in hospital and she told me I'd be out within a week. So I went straight down to the canteen and ate some cream buns, but it didn't do any good – I was out of the hospital in five days. I asked about getting back to the battalion but they said that I had to go to Convalescent (Con.) Depot first. I didn't see the need after only five days but they said that everyone had to go. To add insult to injury (in my opinion the greatest insult I suffered in my army career), they sent a full corporal along to the station with me who waited until the train pulled out to make sure I didn't disappear into the fleshpots of Cairo. No wonder they needed so many people for base jobs.

It was a fair journey to No. 2 Con. Depot at El Ballah, near Nantara (El Qantara) on the Suez Canal. The train went via Cairo, Zagazig, Tel El Kebir, Qassassin, and Ismailia, passing through many small villages, with the oxen at their endless circuits of the wells pulling up water for the irrigation ditches. We were plagued by pedlars at every station offering eggs, bread, fruit and lemonade. 'Very good, George, very cheap' (every squaddy was George to them), but risky to one's health. When we got off and walked into the Con. Depot I found another health risk – gangs of squaddies throwing telegraph poles about. I thought I must have come to the wrong place and tried to get out but they insisted that I stayed. Luckily I managed to dodge most of it. To start with one didn't have to do anything until one had seen the MO. He only came round once a week and we had just missed him, so that took care of the first six days (I was there a fortnight in all). Then we also had to see the dentist and he found enough to do to enable me to duck out of the rest of the exertions. In fact I only had one day's exercise during the two weeks. I shared a tent with a corporal in the military police, a bombardier from an anti-tank regiment and a private from the Green Howards. There was quite a good library and we spent the time reading, at the NAAFI and going to the pictures.

At the end of the two weeks I went off to the Infantry Base Depot at Geneifa, also on the Canal, by train via Ismailia, Fayid and Fanara. Geneifa was a vast city of tents close to the Canal; it was curious to look across the desert and see masts and funnels moving slowly along. On reaching No. 5 Company (the Rifle Brigade Company) I was cheered to find about half a dozen chaps from my own platoon, mostly recovering from wounds received at Alamein, and another dozen from other platoons in the company. They were already on a draft back to the battalion. It is curious that no matter how scared one was, nor how uncomfortable life could be in the desert, most people could not wait to get back to the battalion. Despite the safety and relative comfort of the Delta, the battalion was 'home', where all one's friends were. It was almost as if the people were of two different races – those who lived 'up the sharp end', and the 'base-wallahs'. This was soon illustrated when I went to the office to book in. The lance corporal there, looking at my stripe, said 'You can take that off now' (the rank of lance corporal was a local one only effective within one's own unit). I replied, 'Ah but battle casualties keep their rank.' I wasn't a battle casualty but he wasn't to know that and I wanted to hang on to it to keep me away from fatigues, etc. Besides, he had annoyed me. I said, 'Don't worry, I'm not after your job, I only want to get on that draft back to the 1st Battalion.' He cheered up at that but said I would have to see the MO first. Next morning, having been cleared by the MO, I returned to the office, but they then said that I couldn't go 'up the desert' until I'd been on a hardening course, which involved leaping over ditches, climbing walls, clambering along ropes, etc. I told them I'd had a year in the desert and didn't need hardening, and anyway I'd just spent two weeks being hardened after only a few days in hospital. But it didn't make any difference and so I had to start the course. Luckily Christmas was coming and the course was abbreviated – I only had three days and on Christmas Eve I managed to wangle my name on the draft. I had been scared stiff it would go off without me, in which case I would probably be caught for a draft to one of our other battalions. We spent our spare time at the NAAFI and at Shafto's cinema, which was a tented affair where they occasionally put the film on upside down and there was a five-minute break when they changed the reel. With everyone busy cheering the hero and booing the villain and the usual shouts of 'look behind you' it was quite a bit of fun. The food was much better than desert fare too, and on Christmas Day we had turkey and Christmas pudding.

Christmas Day 1942

At the moment I'm just lying in the tent recovering from our Christmas dinner, which was better than I expected. Turkey, pork, baked potatoes, greens, sausage stuffing, apple sauce, followed by Xmas pudding, custard and jelly, and also beer, ginger beer, cigarettes, an orange and a banana!

I only hope the lads with the company had a good time too …

The Russians still seem to be doing wonders, in spite of the bad weather. Jerry won't be feeling very happy by the time spring arrives. I think this is the brightest Christmas news we have had since the war started.

Just think, in another three months I shall become time-expired or 'time-ex' as they call it, four years since I signed on the dotted line – it seems more like 40! I can see that when I get home it will be difficult to shift from the fireside.

We are all thinking of the folks at home, and wondering what they are doing, and whether or not it will be over by next year. Everyone has become an amateur strategist and has his own pet theory for the quickest way of getting to Berlin.

On Boxing Day we were up at 3 am to get the train across the Delta via Tel al Kebir, Zagazig and Tanta to Amriya, outside Alex, where we arrived at six in the evening. We spent three days at the transit camp and then another 3 am departure, by cattle truck this time, to the docks where we boarded the Princess Kathleen, a Canadian Pacific ferry in peacetime. We were packed like sardines for the two-day trip to Benghazi and we lived on tins of bully and tea. We would have been a choice target for a U-boat but we had three corvettes to escort us. We reached Benghazi on the morning of 31 December and had a four-mile march to the transit camp. We were fast asleep at midnight when we were woken by light AA fire; the sky was full of tracers from Bofors and machine guns, and we were out of the tents and halfway to the slit trenches when someone shouted, 'Come back, it's only the New Year.' The next four days we spent bumping around in RASC (Royal Army Service Corps) third and second line transport chasing the battalion westwards, through Agedabia, El Agheila, Marble Arch and Nofilia, finishing up in a Field Maintenance Centre where we had to go on the scrounge for rations whilst they tried to find out where the battalion was. We eventually found we had overrun them – they were back near Marble Arch, out in the desert, and I finally got back to B Company on 6 January having been away for six weeks (but with only five days of that spent in hospital). They had not had much excitement in that time but had now changed back to being an anti-tank company again, this time with no portees. We had to tow the 6-pounders with 3-tonners. They were up to strength again, although still short of officers, two of the platoons being commanded by sergeants, including ours. I was promoted to full corporal immediately on my return.

January 1943

I'm very pleased to be back again with the boys and have been feeling more cheerful the last couple of days than I have been for months, singing like a lark all day!

We had a sing song last night, and I couldn't help smiling at the sight of the mixed nature of the company – a bank clerk, lorry driver, painter, commercial artist, shop assistant and a road mender, all bellowing at the top of their voices all the songs you can think of ...

...News still seems to be good, things should look pretty bright by the spring, and I don't think it will be very long now before the end comes in sight.

The final push to Tripoli was due to start in a week's time, and over that period we moved forward by stages the 200 miles to Buerat, where the Afrika Korps had taken up a position on the Wadi Zemzem after withdrawing from El Agheila. We set off on the 15th and apart from an initial flurry of shells before Jerry pulled back we had a peaceful progress for the next few days. Our brigade had been detached from the division and was moving up between the 7th Armoured and New Zealand Divisions in the desert on our left, and the Highland Division on the coast road on our right. The Highlanders found the most difficulty because of all the mines and demolitions on the road. We eventually joined the coast road at Zliten and followed it through Homs and towards Tripoli. It was very hilly here and vehicles could not get off the road, so a colossal traffic jam developed, with our brigade and the Highland Division trying to get forward at the same time. Luckily the traffic was all one way, but even so we moved in fits and starts. First we would be stopped and a lot of Highland Division trucks would go past, then they would stop and we would overtake them, with a certain amount of backchat every time. On one occasion, in the middle of the night as we were driving past, their trucks suddenly started up and both columns were driving side by side along the somewhat narrow road. A few ripe words were exchanged when the truck alongside nearly bumped into us and a pure cockney voice came out of the darkness, 'Oos that, the ruddy RBs?' The only non-Scottish unit in the Highland Division was their machine gun battalion, the Middlesex, so I said, 'Yes. Who's that, the Middlesex?' Whereupon the answer came back, 'Middlesex be blowed – we're the Argyll and Suvverland 'Ighlanders'. This somewhat shook my faith in the purity of the Highland Division. The road had been blown wherever there was a culvert and as there was no way round the holes had to be filled in as quickly as possible. So we went forward on foot with picks and shovels, shovelled earth into the hole until it was made passable, then jumped on the first vehicles and moved on to repeat the process, so we were pretty tired by the time we got out of the hills.

January 1943

We haven't had much time for cooking lately but we managed to make a roly-poly the other day, which made a change from fried bully and biscuits. In answer to your query, each vehicle does its own cooking, which means groups of from two to six chaps together – we are six at the moment.

I suppose you will be reading in the papers just now the news that we are moving forward once more. Everything seems to be going well, in spite of the huge distances to be covered. It was pointed out to us the other day that the distance between Cairo and Tripoli is the same as that between London and Moscow. We have been getting the news pretty well lately on the whole. We have picked quite a pleasant spot to stop for the moment. I am writing this under the shade of a tree; there is a plantation of them here. Every few minutes a party of Arabs turn up offering eggs and chickens in exchange for tea or sugar – unfortunately, the latter are too scarce to barter away like that. They also scrounge biscuits and cigarettes – if we let them all have some we'd be starving ourselves.

The Germans did not attempt to hold Tripoli and at first light on 23 January the 11th Hussars entered from the south. Finding no enemy they settled down to breakfast in the main square, much to the surprise of the inhabitants when they woke up and emerged from their houses. We could not continue the advance until supplies had caught up, so we settled down for a rest in a grove of palm trees a few miles south of the town. We were woken up at midnight a couple of days later to fill in a large crater in the road from Tarhuna which had been blown up by a delayed action mine.

January 1943

Well we made it at last, and now Musso is talking about the successful evacuation of Tripoli without fighting. It's certainly been a long, long trail, and it's still going on. Of course letters take a long time to reach us these days, and at the moment I could certainly do with some of those parcels of cigarettes. The only thing that is plentiful is water, which is quite a change anyway. I had a bath this morning (in a petrol tin) and did a bit of washing, so feel somewhat cleaner than usual.

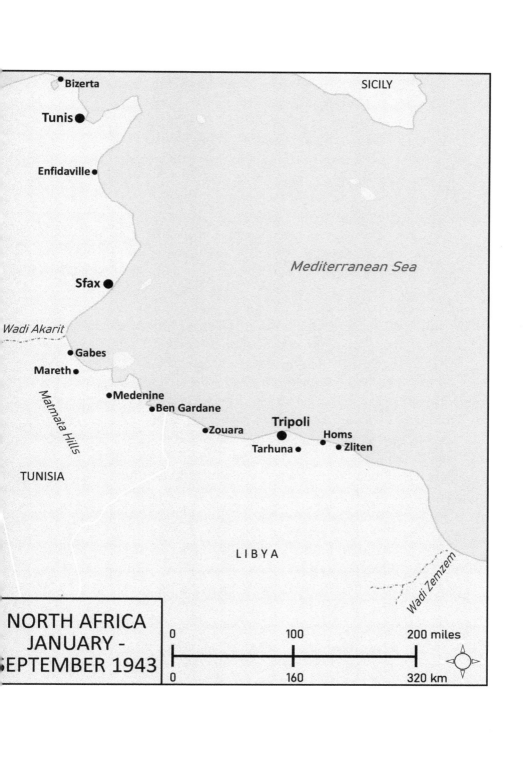

Bizerta

SICILY

Tunis

Enfidaville

Mediterranean Sea

Sfax

Wadi Akarit

Gabes

Mareth

Matmata Hills

Medenine

Ben Gardane

Zouara

Tripoli

Homs

Tarhuna

Zliten

TUNISIA

LIBYA

Wadi Zemzem

NORTH AFRICA
JANUARY -
SEPTEMBER 1943

0	100	200 miles
0	160	320 km

We have also been able to get some green vegetables, cauliflower, peas, etc., so we shall be able to have a change tonight instead of just taking out the bully and saying 'fried or cold?'

We have still got our company wireless set, so we're able to hear the news every night and also some of the ordinary programmes. All that you have to do is to forget that you're squatting round a truck on petrol cans and it's just like being at home!

The news has certainly been pretty good all round lately, and it looks as if the Jerries at Stalingrad are 'in the bag'.

We were very sorry to hear about the air raids on London – it came as a surprise after such a long time, and I hope there won't be any more.

We stayed in the area for about three weeks. Churchill turned up halfway through, so we had a certain amount of drill and cleaning up in anticipation. We were lining the route instead of marching past, which probably saved us a few hours more drill. They don't usually like the Rifle Brigade joining in a march past, as our fast pace upsets everyone else. We occupied ourselves with a certain amount of gun drill, maintenance etc., and some lectures. One of our sections was indulging in some unofficial revolver shooting at tin cans one morning when a staff car pulled up and out stepped our new brigadier, 'Looney' Hinde, a 15th-19th Hussar, and asked if he could join in.[4] He insisted that there must be a prize, so a biscuit was suggested. He duly won the 'competition' and got back into his staff car chewing his army biscuit. We had one day's leave in Tripoli to have a look round. There wasn't much to see except for the wrecked shipping in the harbour including an Italian hospital ship. Whilst we were here the mail that had been following us around ever since I went into hospital finally caught up with me and I had 30 letters in one day.

---

[4]   Later Major General Sir Robert N. Hinde, KBE, CB, DSO 2 bars. The nickname 'Looney' is said to be a tribute to his courage and eccentricity.

February 1943

> *You will be very pleased to hear that your second parcel Sept. 24th arrived safely on the 6th. Thanks so much for the gloves and helmet, and also for the books …*
>
> *… Out here everything is progressing as usual, I suppose as soon as the 1st Army gets debogged in Tunisia things will start livening up again there. As it is the Air Force must be making things very uncomfortable for Jerry, with the planes from Malta taking a hand in it as well.*
>
> *Everyone has supreme confidence in 'Monty'. I've never seen anything like it before.*
>
> *On all sides all you hear is 'How much longer?' 'When will we be demobbed?' 'What will they do in Germany?' and questions of that sort, and odds are being given (and taken) freely, on the chance of it being over by next Christmas. The usual comment on the news bulletin is 'Good old Joe – still going strong!' …*
>
> *… We are now able to tell you that we saw 'Winnie' [Churchill] when he came over the other day – he looked very smart in his Air Force uniform and seemed very pleased with the turnout. He does manage to get about a bit, doesn't he?*
>
> *We have had some very interesting talks lately on the present situation – we are kept very well informed these days as to what is happening, and so forth – it makes a lot of difference, and is a great improvement on the old days, when we were told Sweet Fanny Adams! All we heard were rumours.*

We moved off again on 8 February along the road to Zouara, then out into the desert and across the border into Tunisia (French North Africa) south of Ben Gardane, and into a sandstorm which was followed by rain. We shuttled round in this area for about ten days trying to frighten Jerry out of his positions. Then there was an appeal for help from the 1st Army, where Rommel was chasing the Americans back in great haste, so we moved forward to capture Medenine and close up to the Mareth Line. We set off at first light on 20 February, taking advantage of a ground mist which sheltered us from enemy view. As the temperature rose this started to clear and we came under

A good load!

very heavy shellfire from the high ground to our left, during which my old friend Tom Gray was unlucky enough to lose an eye. We rapidly went to ground, but the shelling continued all day and I had another narrow squeak. I was making a brew, standing by the fire waiting for the water to boil. As it was coming up I walked round to the front of the truck to get the tea out of the ration box when a shell burst slap in the brew can – I had moved just in time.

February 1943

I would have written sooner, but we've been rather active lately and I haven't had much time

The country we are in these days is very different to what it used to be. I am actually writing this sitting in the shade of a tree (the sun gets quite warm in the afternoons now) and there is plenty of grass and cultivated land about, there is also a good bit of water about too.

We can't make up our minds which we dislike least – the heat and flies of summer, or cold and rain of winter. I don't know whether it's worse to get oneself and blankets soaking wet in winter, or lie under a truck sweating and trying to brush the flies off in summer!

I hope some mail comes up with the rations tonight, I should also be getting some more of the cigarettes and parcels you sent but of course they have such a long journey to go now, that they are bound to take longer.

For the next six weeks we occupied various defensive positions facing the Mareth Line. Sometimes it was quiet, sometimes noisy, particularly when Rommel made his unsuccessful attempt to push us back on 6 March. We were in reserve behind the Guards and did not get involved apart from being shelled. We also had an uncomfortable time whenever we were in position on a hill called Abdullah, which was in full view from the Matmata Hills, particularly when the colonel came up for a look and stood on the skyline. The resulting barrage, after he had gone, cost C Company one killed and two wounded, nearly did for us in our gun pit and wounded one of our sergeants. This led to my being transferred to take over his section as No. 1. It was also sticky at the time the 50th Division made their unsuccessful frontal attack on the Mareth Line, when we also had quite a lot of night bombing. There was a lot of aerial activity during the day and many dogfights between Me's and Spits. Then we had to go back to workshops for a new engine, and whilst we were away the battalion was given a sticky job capturing a hill called Jabal Saikra. The two attacking companies could only put about 60 men on the ground and about one-third became casualties, both company commanders being killed. Our company was not closely involved, apart from being heavily shelled.

March 1943

I'm sorry I have not had a chance to write before, but as you will know by the news, things are on the move again out here once more. We are on the last lap now and it won't take very long. I haven't been able to hear the news lately, but gather that things have settled down a bit in Russia, due to the thaw.

I was very interested in the papers that arrived, a lot of the other chaps had some as well, so were able to pass them round. There will be some more up soon. It is funny reading news four months old but still, better late than never, at that time we were too busy to read papers.

Another four days and my four years will be up – it feels more like 40! Still, I suppose it won't last forever.

By now the New Zealanders and the 1st Armoured Division had, thanks to the Long Range Desert Group who had found a route through country that had been considered impassable, made a wide sweep through the desert to the west. They were threatening the Gabes Gap, forcing the Germans to withdraw from the Mareth Line and fall back to the Wadi Akarit. Our 7th Battalion, formerly the 1st London Rifle Brigade, had a bad time here. They had pushed forward and seized a pass which would have enabled the army to penetrate the Akarit position without a pitched battle. But they had advanced beyond the range of the field guns and when they called for support from the medium battery they had been promised, they found it had been moved elsewhere, added to which the armour was too late arriving. After five hours of heavy counter attack they were forced to pull back, losing 150 men. Meanwhile we motored through the foothills and waited for the infantry to make a gap in the Akarit position. The attack went in on 6 April, and after a night when the Luftwaffe again appeared to bomb and strafe us, we went through the gap made by the Highland Division next morning. The Black Watch had a hard time and in places the bodies were lying in extended order. We made about twenty miles that day and another twenty the next, reaching the Mahares-Maknassy railway where their rearguard decided we had gone far enough for a day. We had a go at four Mark IVs but I think their shots got closer to us than ours to them.

Next day we had some fun. We were travelling in regimental groups – that is, our platoon with C Company and a battery of guns were with the 1st Royal Tanks. On the move we tagged along behind the tanks unless and until their colonel called us forward. By now we had left the desert and were travelling through olive groves and small copses. After we had gone some way the column stopped and from the noises ahead we deduced that our tanks had bumped his rearguard again.

Suddenly our platoon commander put his blue flag up and moved forward. He was a brand-new chico (subaltern) straight out from England and had already caused problems because he couldn't wake up in the morning. When in close leaguer it was essential to open out at first light to avoid being spotted and shelled whilst we were still nose to tail, but on at least one occasion we had had to pull away leaving him still lying in his sleeping bag with his driver frantically trying to get him up. Anyway, we moved forward in a somewhat uncertain manner with stops and ever-increasing zig-zags until eventually he turned sharp right. He made off eastwards towards where, in the distance, we could see the 23rd Armoured Brigade who were working with the Highland Division having their own private battle with part of the German rearguard. He went up to one of the tanks (they were equipped with Valentines), had a few words and came away again. By now I was a bit concerned so I went up and asked him what he was up to. He said we had been called forward by the 1st Tanks but he couldn't find them. I said 'What the … have you come over here for – can't you tell the difference between a Valentine and a Sherman?' I pointed out where the tank battle was going on between the 1st Tanks and the Germans and he set off back. After a time we came to the lip of a valley in which the battle was going on, with the British tanks on our left and the Germans on our right. We couldn't see much because of the olives, but one could tell from the tracers; the British were red and the Germans white. To our amazement he set off down in the direction of the Germans instead of the British. We decided there was no future in following him so we all stopped where we were to see the fun. A Cherrypicker (11th Hussars) armoured car was nearby, came over and asked where he had gone. When we told him he said 'He'll be back in a couple of minutes. I've just been shelled out of there.' Sure enough in a couple of minutes he came back, following a few loud bangs, and we told him in a few choice words what we thought of him. By now it was twilight and it was getting difficult to see anyone, but by luck we managed to bump into our own Company HQ and spent the night with them. I don't know how big a rocket he got but they took him away and found odd jobs for him and eventually got him transferred to the Free French as a liaison officer. Our officers varied, some very good, some not as good, but we never had another one like him. How he got through OCTU I'll never know.

Next day we moved forward a bit further until we were eight miles west of Sfax and settled down for a couple of days maintenance. We were supposed to be going into reserve and were just cleaning up for a divisional commander's inspection when suddenly, as ever, everything was changed and we moved 80 miles north to Kairouan, the Holy City. We sat down again a few miles to the north and for the first time had a sight of the 1st Army and the Americans. I think the reason for the sudden change was that the 1st Armoured Division was being sent round to help the 1st Army and we were called up to replace them in X Corps for the attack on the Enfidaville line.

April 1943

Of course you've heard by now that the 8th Army are beyond Sousse and on the last lap – I don't think it will take very long though it will be a tough job while it lasts. The RAF are certainly putting 'em through it good and proper.

The ration strength of our section has now increased to nine, as the result of the acquisition of three pullets, which we hope will eventually be induced to lay eggs, if we keep them long enough! It's a comic sight, when we get a sudden order to move, to see gangs of people rushing about with sticks and rifles, diving under trucks, trying to round up the poultry before we go.

I was very surprised to find herds of cattle as well as sheep round here. There is plenty of water about and the whole country is green, instead of half desert as before. I don't think I told you that about a month ago I came to another section – they are a very good crowd – some of the best I have been with, although I've never been with them before.

After nearly a week we moved into position near Djebel Fadeloun, spending most of the night digging in. We came under occasional shellfire but were more at risk from the prickly cactus bushes with which the ground was covered. I had one bad moment when one of

Hetty and Ethel want a ride!   *Hetty and Ethel on our gun*

our chaps spotted a stray horse which was roaming around and decided to go for a ride bareback. As soon as he mounted it took off for the German lines at a rate of knots, but luckily he gradually managed to turn it round and got back safely. It was here that we acquired our two hens, Hetty and Ethel, from some Arabs. Unfortunately they failed to keep us supplied with more than the occasional egg, but we kept them for some months until we went to Italy. They then went in the pot, but none of us had the heart to eat them, so they were eaten by one of the other sections. After about a week the enemy had withdrawn from our front, but were still holding on to our right where attacks by the Indians and New Zealanders had been only partially successful. It was decided that the 8th Army would not persist in its offensive but would help the 1st Army in its attack on Tunis. We pulled back to a concentration area and three days later our division, with the Indians, set off on the long trek to join the 1st Army.

We left on the night of 30 April, covering 50 miles during the night through Kairouan and another 50 miles next day through Ousseltia. Another twenty miles the following day brought us into the thick of the 1st Army. In some ways it was rather like meeting a foreign army; in

On the move – Tunisia, April 1943

fact we used to call them the 'Inglese'. They all wore battledress with equipment and steel helmets and their vehicles were dark green and brown, as they were in England. The 8th Army, on the other hand, had operated as a sort of private army for up to three years. The officers usually wore corduroy trousers, suede boots and pullovers of various shades. We wore khaki drill in various styles, often with coloured scarves. No one wore a tin hat unless it was absolutely necessary. Discipline was fairly relaxed because we did our fighting in small groups of three to six men, and teamwork and reliance on one's mates was more important than anything else. We spoke a language that (when it was printable) was so interlarded with Arabic plus bits of Hindustani, Maltese and other languages as to be almost unintelligible. Our vehicles were a light sandy colour, hung around with cooking pots and brew-cans. There were odd incidents, as when Redcaps on traffic duty tried to check our chaps for being improperly dressed and were told where they got off. We didn't help by being sarcastic about their performance, pointing out that we were at

Near the Enfidaville Line – Tunisia 1943

Prisoners on the Tunis road – May 1943

Alamein when they landed and had advanced 2,000 miles to find that they were still outside Tunis. This was unfair, as it was due in no small part to their being called 'an army' when for a considerable time their strength was little more than two divisions – a fact of which of course we were unaware at the time.

We now started getting our rations from the 1st Army in the form of 'compo packs', cardboard boxes containing enough for fourteen men for one day. There were seven different versions, marked from A to G (presumably the idea was to have a different one for each day of the week, but we didn't receive them like that). A was the favourite because it contained steak and kidney pudding and tinned fruit. 'E' was the bottom of the list because we were not keen on haricot oxtail. But there were the usual distribution problems for the poor old platoon sergeant. If there were four sets of six, one of three and one of two, how does one split up four Compo boxes plus a few odd tins for two days? To ensure fair play we had to open the boxes and distribute on a rota basis, not only so far as the main items were concerned but also so that everyone got their fair share of jam, cheese, etc. We found that the rations were lavish compared with what we were used to and soon built up quite a stock of meat and veg. A daily ration of sweets and chocolate was something new, but we were not keen on the tea/sugar/milk powder, preferring the traditional brew. The boxes also contained seven cigarettes a man. These compo packs were also what we lived on in Normandy and afterwards.

After a couple of days we moved forward to the concentration area for the final attack on Tunis. We were to break through after the 4th Indian Division had made a gap, with two of the 1st Army Divisions doing the same thing on our right. We were not looking forward to it because the German defences in this area had always been strong and we were no longer in the desert but in a country of hills and woods with much less visibility. In the event it was a piece of cake. We spent the night near Medjez el Bab and first thing next morning moved up through the Indians, who had done the job so well that there was no enemy in sight. We moved forward slowly all day and by nightfall we were only sixteen miles from Tunis. This we covered the following day

Gun drill (Ken on the left) – Homs, summer 1943

with only sporadic opposition from tanks and anti-tank guns. By 4 pm we were in the outskirts of Tunis where we received a great welcome from the French. This was briefly interrupted when we shot up a stray German staff car containing a very truculent Nazi officer who was rapidly taken down a peg or two. As usual we weren't to go into the city. Instead we shot across country to cut off the troops retreating from Bizerta towards Tunis. It all ended peacefully, except for us being bombed by the US Air Force. That was partly our fault because we had advanced beyond our bombing line but even so they ignored the yellow smoke we let off in clouds to tell them where we were. The Germans gave up when they found the bridge over the river blown and us sitting on the far bank. Part of the army spent the next few days persuading the remaining Germans and Italians in the Cape Bon peninsula to pack up, but for us the campaign was over.

It had been a long haul – 2,000 miles in the last six months – and we'd had nearly a year up and down 'the Blue' before that, some had two or two and a half years. Our battalion had not left the desert for a rest or a refit for the whole eighteen months, and I have not been able to trace any other infantry battalion or armoured regiment that did the same, although there may have been some gunner regiments who never went back. It was a very different battalion from the one which had arrived eighteen months before, and there were only a couple of handfuls of us still in B Company.

May 1943

I'm sorry I haven't written sooner, but as you can guess we've had a very busy time lately, getting rid of the Afrika Korps. It was a far easier job than we ever expected – he was strained to the uttermost, and only wanted that final crack to finish him off altogether. The prisoners (they are 90% Jerries) have been swarming in in hundreds, coming in quite on their own, with no one to look after them!

You will have heard on the wireless who reached Tunis first – the old Desert Rat has already become familiar to the French people. They had anything but a pleasant time while Jerry was there, and there is no doubt they really are pleased to see us. I have got a copy of the first number of 'Tunis Telegraph' specially produced for the troops, dated May 10th. I will keep it to show you when I get home.

I've had to polish up my French a bit lately as very few of the people speak any English, but we've been getting along very well so far, and we can usually make ourselves understood.

We have soon got back to the old routine again – drills, parades, etc. I was orderly sergeant yesterday!

There's been plenty of Canteen about lately, a lot of cigarettes, and today I even had a bar of Rowntree's Chocolate Cream!

May 1943

Well, it's all over at last, as you will have heard on the wireless tonight, we can hardly realise it ourselves. It seems impossible that the days of chasing up and down the desert between Alamein and Agheila are over. At any rate there's a certain amount of satisfaction in finishing off the job properly, and in paying off some old scores of the Knightsbridge days and earlier.

Of course, no one knows what we shall do next, but we are all hoping for a spot of rest before they find any more trouble for us.

Vic and Bud with a Fiat - Homs, June 1943

Drawing water – Homs, June 1943

We did not stay for the victory celebrations in Tunis, although they did give us a day's leave to have a look round and to enjoy the welcome of the French people. We moved 50 miles south for a few days, which we spent cleaning up and doing drill parades. Then we went right back the way we had come, through the Mareth Line and round Tripoli, taking five days to do 600 miles and finishing on the beach six miles east of Homs, where we were to spend the next four months. It was an ideal spot underneath the palm trees, with just the beach between us and the sea, which was a blessing in the scorching heat. This compensated for a return to non-operational routine of gun drill, weapon training, drill parades (including battalion ceremonial parades), lectures, route marches, firing 6-pounders and small arms and maintenance. We went back to a company cookhouse instead of doing our own cooking. We were able to enjoy a swim in the Med morning and evening and the little Arab girls, Fatima and Howa, did our washing. It was much more pleasant than living in barracks. We were inspected by the divisional commander, who told us, much to our sorrow, that there would be no leave to the Delta (there was leave to Tripoli, but not much to do there) and there would be a job for us to do later in the summer. This did not surprise us as we had not expected them to allow us to rest on our laurels for the rest of the war. There followed an inspection by the King who had come out to see the army. Immediately afterwards (although it wasn't his doing) I was promoted to sergeant. I was told at first it was to be lance sergeant, but was made a full sergeant straight away which helped my pay, not that there was much to spend it on – we were able to save most of it until we got home. I spent a week on a mines and explosives course learning how to lift mines, hopefully without blowing oneself up, and how to cause a big bang with a bit of explosive and some fuse. Luckily I only had to put this knowledge to use once, in Normandy, to clear a lot of mines from where we wanted to put our gun pit. We also went to Tripoli once or twice to practice boarding landing craft and making 'wet' landings.

Charlie frying the Bully – summer 1943

Down where the watermelons grow – Homs, August 1943

August 1943

> *Thank you so much for the POs, cigs and all the birthday greetings. Luckily we got a bottle of beer each yesterday so I was able to celebrate a bit.*
>
> *The weather is still about the same, ditto the flies, still we're half way through August now and before we know where we are it will be winter again. I wonder where we shall spend the winter this year? This time last year I was just about to go on leave and got back just in time for Rommel's push – things looked a bit different then.*
>
> *I see you have read about the 'Africa Star'. We're rather disappointed in it, as it seems that any old Tom, Dick or Harry in a cushy job, who's never even heard a gun fired, will get one, whilst some of the chaps who've earned them most, like the seamen who used to take the Malta Convoys through, will not get them.*

We were not called on for the Sicilian campaign, but on 3 September the 8th Army landed on the toe of Italy and on the 9th the 5th Army (called American, but in fact half British) landed at Salerno, which was our destination. We started packing up the next day but there were a number of delays because the battle at Salerno was not going well. There was talk of re-embarkation at one stage but the Guards Brigade got ashore and an American airborne division was parachuted in and they restored the situation. We moved to Tripoli on the 15th but didn't finally board the landing craft until the 19th, when we shook off the dust of Africa and sailed at 6.30 pm aboard the US LST 312.

Italy

❦

The three-day voyage to Salerno in a convoy of two LSTs passing Mount Etna and through the Straits of Messina was uneventful with a calm sea. As usual we lived on bully and biscuits and we were somewhat envious on this occasion, watching the American sailors going to the galley for their food to hear one complain, 'Aw, gee, not fried chicken again.' We arrived off Salerno on the morning of the 22nd, by which time the bridgehead was secure and there was only one gun firing random shells into the bay. We messed about all day, making three attempts to get ashore and grounding on a sandbank on one occasion. We eventually pulled onto the beach at about 6 pm. Luckily it was a dry landing – the ramp went down on the beach, not in the water – and we moved off to an orchard near Battipaglia which was our assembly area, and where we joined up with the 1st Tanks, with whom we were to operate.

September 1943 Battipaglia, Italy

I'm glad the parcel arrived safely, I ordered it at Sfax over five months ago.

You will notice the new address we've got, Central Mediterranean Force. I suppose you will guess what that means. At any rate we're not sorry to get away from the Middle East after the last two years, and of course we are a bit nearer home now. I expect you were pleased to hear about Italy's surrender. Of course Jerry is still making a scrap of it, but it makes a lot of difference not having the Iti's to help him.

The Russians are having a big go for Smolensk and Kiev too. I wonder if they'll get there before the rains

There was a delay of six days whilst 46 Div. cleared the mountains north of Salerno so that we could pass through and break out into the

Naples plain. The weather was wet and as we were in mosquito country we had to take mepacrine tablets every day and keep our sleeves rolled down at night; not that it stopped us getting bitten, but not many people contracted malaria. One of the things we did to pass the time was to dig in and camouflage our guns, then get the tank crews to try and spot them so that they could get some idea of what it would be like in Europe instead of Africa. One bunch were more than horrified when I stepped out from behind a gun and said 'Boo' when they were only about ten yards away – it made them think a bit.

We finally moved off at first light on 28 September and promptly slid into the ditch and got stuck in the mud, and it was evening before we could catch up our own place in the column. The divisional column was 55 miles long on one road. We continued moving forward very slowly for the next two days. The 'King's Dancing Girls' (King's Dragoon Guards) in their armoured cars had managed to capture the bridge over the River Sarno at Scafati but there was tremendous congestion as the various units got across and pushed forward on the other side. The 23rd Armoured Brigade veered west for Naples but we turned east and made our way round Vesuvius before turning north. Many of the villages had been badly battered but the Italian people gave us a big welcome. We did not take too kindly to this, because we had been fighting them for three years, after they had joined in when they had thought it was nearly all over in the hope of some cheap gains (Nice, Corsica, Tunis). Looking back I think this was unfair because the ordinary Italian people had never wanted the war, and they certainly had no love for the Germans. Anyway, they kept pressing bottles of wine on us (it tasted like vinegar) and then promptly asked for cigarettes. Quite a lot spoke American having spent some time there, or they had relatives there, and a few had lived in London, mainly waiters. There was never a fascist among them. The children were always badgering us for 'biscotti' or 'cigarette for Papa', and whenever we were cooking and eating we rapidly attracted an audience of both children and adults who watched every move and jabbered away to one another in a form of running commentary. It took a bit of getting used to, after the solitude of the desert.

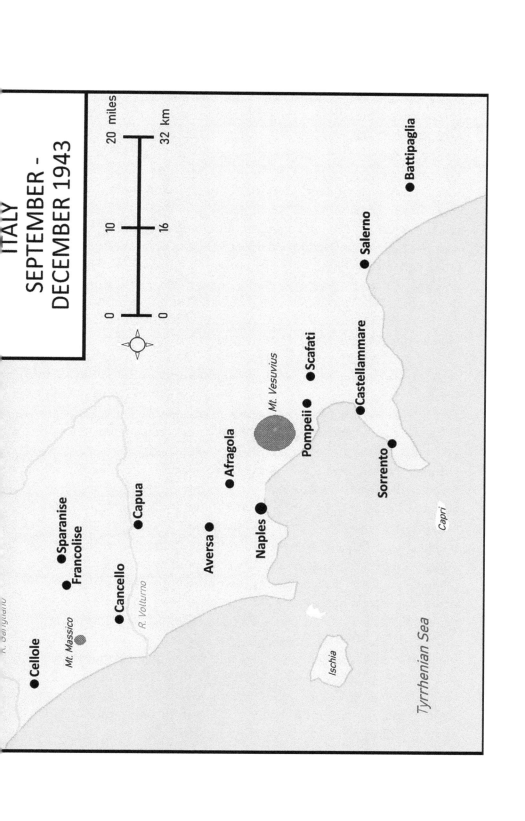

ITALY
SEPTEMBER -
DECEMBER 1943

20 miles
10
0

32 km
16
0

● Battipaglia

● Salerno

● Castellammare

Scafati ●

Pompeii ●

Mt. Vesuvius

● Afragola

Sorrento ●

● Naples

● Aversa

● Capua

Cancello ●

R. Volturno

Sparanise ●
Francolise ●

Mt. Massico

● Cellole

R. Garigliano

Capri

Ischia

Tyrrhenian Sea

We pushed on through heavy rain, through Somma Vesuviana to Casalnuovo where we got caught by Nebelwerfer as we were about to take up positions blocking the Naples road. The Nebelwerfer was a six-barrelled mortar commonly known as 'Adolph's Organ' or 'Moaning Minnie' because of the moaning noise rather like a siren which started slowly and gradually increased to a crescendo. As the barrels were fired one after the other and they operated in batteries of six, one received 36 bombs almost simultaneously over a very small area. We had just pulled into a field with no trenches or other cover, but amazingly escaped with only the mother-truck driver being wounded and the platoon sergeant's greatcoat being riddled with shrapnel. But during the shelling that followed, one of 6 Platoon's sections suffered a direct hit, killing two and wounding four. We then moved forward to a village called Afragola where we spent the night in a sunken road being shelled periodically. I always thought that shelling at night was worse than during the day because one could see the flash of the explosions, whereas during the day one could see only the smoke; the lack of visibility also seemed to make it more unpleasant.

Next morning the advance was held up at a village named Cardito and C Company's two motor platoons were sent in to clear it, but within three minutes a third of their 40 men had become casualties from shelling and mortaring on the start line. In the close country the Germans were able to get their OPs up very close and bring down accurate fire when needed. In the afternoon I Company came up and, taking a route through some closer country, succeeded in clearing the village. There was a suggestion that we should take part in the attack, on foot, with the carriers taking our guns up behind us so that we could man them against a counter attack once we had cleared the village, but luckily the idea was dropped – perhaps they thought they might finish up with all the guns but no gunners. We moved up to block a crossroads near the village and once again came under very heavy observed fire. I dived behind one of the Sherman tanks that we were relieving, but he started reversing out of it, so I nipped under a steam roller that was standing by the side of the road, only to find an elderly Italian already there. He was carrying a set of (British) webbing equipment and had a large kitchen knife between his teeth. Not knowing whose side, if any, he was on, I relieved him of both. Luckily no one was hit, except an Italian seaman who, for some reason, was walking along the road.

Next day we moved forward to Aversa and on to Fertilia and the following morning went across the Regi Lagni Canal towards the River Volturno, passing through an ammunition dump in which the stacks of shells were going off at intervals, which was somewhat alarming. After a day near the river we moved back to Aversa for a fortnight whilst supplies were brought up for the next stage of the advance, which would start by forcing the river crossing. We were billeted in the tram terminus and at first life was made hideous by the troops clanging the bells on the trams, but eventually they got tired of it.

October 1943

Well, we are now allowed to mention that we are in Italy, although not, of course, whereabouts or in which army. We are finding it very strange having all these people around us all the time, instead of a barren desert.

They are very demonstrative, especially when we go in one end of a village as Jerry is clearing out the other end – it's rather disconcerting to go down the street with much hand-clapping and showers of fruit, and then turn a corner and receive some of Jerry's best assorted fireworks! Still, there are some advantages, and we often manage to get into some sort of building when it is raining.

At the moment we are parked in a tram terminus! Jerry seems to have made sure no one will use the trams for some time to come, but the bells still seem to clang as heartily as ever.

I remember one small boy coming in, standing by one of the trams and singing all the well-known Italian songs at the top of his voice. We also had the real thing; one of our officers was able to get an opera company from Naples to come and give us a concert. Whilst there we were issued with battledress – about time as it was getting cold in khaki drill even though we had slacks instead of shorts. We took it easy

Ken on motorbike – Scafati, October 1943

for a few days and were able to get a trip into Naples, but our rest was interrupted after a week, when we were turned out late one night and rushed up to the river, where the Sherwood Foresters had got across but been pushed back into the river (literally – many of them were drowned) by a counterattack and our battalion had to plug the gap. After a couple of days we were able to move back to Aversa, at first on standby but later we were able to get into Naples again, including a visit to the airfield to meet the Spitfires of 72 Squadron.

We moved forward again at dawn on 21 October, across the Volturno at Capua and up Highway 7 to a vineyard below Sparanise and Francolise (known to the troops as Sparrer's knees and Frankie's knees) where we relieved a battalion of the Queens from 56 Div. The position was overlooked from the high ground and we once more had to put up with accurate shelling and mortaring from Nebelwerfers; shrapnel punctured one of the tyres of our portee before we could get it back out of harm's way. We had three days of this, during which I Company captured Sparanise, then we moved forward a bit and spent

5 Platoon, 'B' Company. Ken seated third from left – Sorrento, December 1943

the night digging in whilst A and C Companies took Francolise. A day later we were relieved by the Durhams and moved west to the coastal sector where the battalion took up positions on the Agnena Nuova Canal north of Cancello ed Arnone. We had another company reorganisation here. One of our four anti-tank platoons (No. 8) was broken up and the machine gun platoons from the three motor companies were transferred to us and reduced to two. So there was much shifting round of people, with some of our chaps being moved out and being replaced by others from 8 Platoon. Apart from casualties, or sometimes because of casualties, there was a constant movement of men between the sections within the platoon, between the platoons within the company, or sometimes to other companies. The stay of some was short, others remained a long time, with a diminishing band of those who had come out from England with us. There must have been several hundred members of my platoon during my time in it and it is not always easy to remember who was with us at any particular moment. Some I can remember clearly, both in appearance and voice, others are just hazy outlines, whilst some are just names in my diary or old roll-books.

November 1943

You mention about the 'compo rations'; we only get them very occasionally, but they do contain sweets, chocolate and cigarettes – seven Players each. In the ordinary way we only get the old 'V's', otherwise known as 'Desert Players', just about smokeable and usually somewhat stale. Our usual diet is bully and potatoes, of which there are still plenty about, they cost about ten lira a kilo – that is about four and a half pounds for a shilling, so we always have plenty of 'chips and mash'.

We have been a bit disturbed in our meals lately – pelting down the road trying to eat bully and chips – but we hope to get our meal in peace tonight.

Once we were sorted out we moved forward over the canal, beyond which the battalion had by now made a bridgehead. After a couple of days the Queens moved through us and captured Mondragone and

Monte Massico, then we rejoined the 1st Tanks and took up the advance towards the River Garigliano, across which the Germans had withdrawn. After a couple of days blocking the Rome road, on 5 November the colonel came round to tell us we were going home – to be withdrawn into Imperial Strategic Reserve as he termed it. The news seemed incredible at the time and most people said they'd believe it when we got there, and even then there was bound to be a catch in it. Anyway, we would not be sorry to leave Italy, as the cold of the winter was approaching and the mountains (Cassino) loomed ahead. Our other three battalions in the theatre, who were still sunning themselves in the Middle East, eventually found themselves in Italy as 'ordinary' infantry, struggling up and down the mountains on their flat feet, supplied by pack mules. I think on the whole we were better off in the end.

Next day we were relieved by the Lincolns and moved back a few miles where we started cleaning up the guns ready for handing over. But after a couple of days we were called forward again to Cellole about three miles short of the river. Here we dug in for five very nervous days, as no one wanted to cop it just before going home, and people tended to keep very close to their slit trenches. Actually it was very quiet except for one morning when we were very heavily shelled, one landing just beside my slit trench. A Jerry patrol must have come across during the night and spotted our positions. As far as I know the only person in the battalion who lost his life during this period was an officer of I Company who took a patrol across the river and was drowned on the way back.

November 1943

I was interested to hear that the school are doing so well at rugger this year – 212 points to 3 is a pretty good start off. I was sorry to hear about Pat O'Brien, I knew him at school. I am glad you have been getting some 'Tiffinians' school magazines, I hope I'll get a chance to read them some day. Schooldays seem years ago now, actually six years in April.

We were finally relieved on 14 November and returned to our old home in the tram terminus at Aversa, where we spent four days cleaning up and handing our guns, vehicles and equipment to the Canadian Armoured Division. We felt a bit sorry for them because the vehicles had all come through the desert and were long past their best and were no doubt in a much worse state than those they had left in England. On the 19th the RASC took us to Sorrento, where we were billeted in a lemon warehouse for what turned out to be a month waiting for transport home. I think this was longer than anyone expected and they didn't know what to do with us, especially as we had no weapons (other than our rifles) or vehicles to look after. We started off with a week's course of elementary weapon training (recruit stuff) then a bit of drill and PT. Then I had a week as company orderly sergeant. I don't remember whether I had committed some sin to account for this but there was nothing else to do anyway. Sorrento is a very pretty place but there was not much to do in our spare time. Mostly we played cards and tombola. There was no transport to get out of town, nowhere to walk to and it was a bit cold for swimming and sunbathing. Capri was out of bounds except to Americans (of course). One of the main events from my point of view was that an Italian barber who cut my hair managed to put a wave in it. I walked around with my head on one side for the rest of the day but by next morning it had vanished, never to return. There was a steep zig zag path leading down from the town to the seashore and one day we saw an Italian sitting on top of a very, very heavily laden cart and whipping a tiny little donkey to make it pull him up the hill. So we made him get off and help the donkey by pushing the cart from behind all the way to the top. I don't think he could understand what we were making all the fuss about.

At last on 18 December we moved off. To our horror the colonel had apparently declined the offer of transport on the grounds that we were infantry and we had to march the eleven miles to Castellamare in full kit. There was no question of stuffing our packs with paper because we had to get our things home. It was a wonderful scenic road with views of the Bay of Naples, but we were too interested in our sore feet to notice it. We had only had one short march for practice and apart from that we had not walked anywhere for months, so there were plenty of large blisters when we arrived. Next morning we went by cattle truck to Casoria and marched two miles to the transit camp. The company had to march to the docks at 3.45 next morning, but for once I was in luck and travelled by truck as i/c baggage party. We boarded the *Cameronia* (a Cunarder) and sailed at 4 pm on 20 December.

The ship was very crowded, even worse than the *Strathaird*, and we didn't have a very happy trip. The only activities were boat drills and muster parades. A stream of odd rules and regulations was constantly being issued and in my diary I noted 'The CC Troops is mad.' Our food in the Sergeants' Mess was very good, but for the troops it was very poor; their potatoes were always black, whether from mud or because they were bad I don't know. When we made a formal complaint he said, 'Don't you people know there's a war on?' which we thought a bit rich. Every transport had a 'dug-out' lieut-colonel permanently on board as CC Troops. After three days we reached Oran in somewhat spectacular fashion. I looked out of a porthole and saw the jetty racing past at a rate of knots when suddenly there was a grinding noise which lasted for several seconds. We had come in too fast and scraped along the side of the French battleship *Lorraine*, although the damage was not enough to make us unseaworthy. The following day, Christmas Eve, we went on the quay for exercise. The highlight of Christmas Day was a film show – *Life begins for Andy Hardy*. On Boxing Day we went for a route march in pouring rain, and after lunch pulled away from the quay and anchored in the bay, ready to sail first thing the following morning. There were ten transports including the *Mooltan*, *Highland Princess*, *Ormonde* and *Johann de Witt*, with an escort of a light cruiser and about eight destroyers. We passed through the Straits of Gibraltar at 1 am so I didn't see anything of the Rock. It took us eight days to reach the Clyde where we anchored in the Firth early on the morning of 4 January 1944.

Back in England

❦

While we were still off the Tail of the Bank, Jimmy Bosvile, who had been our colonel when we went out to the desert and had come home as a brigadier after the fall of Tunis, came aboard to greet us and put us in the picture. He told us that a fitting welcome awaited us but we didn't realise that he must have had his tongue in his cheek at the time. We were also visited by a customs officer who came down to the mess deck, stood on a table and said, 'Hands up anyone with more than a thousand cigarettes, anyone with more than six pairs of silk stockings, anyone with more than four bottles of whisky?' Receiving no reaction, he said, 'Thanks lads, cheerio,' and disappeared.

After 24 hours at anchor, gazing at the distant shore, we moved up the river and pulled into the King George Dock at 10.30 in the morning. We were all packed up and ready to go but we spent most of the next fourteen hours gazing at a deserted quay before we eventually landed at 1 am on the 6th with an audience of two dockers, three military police and a porter. The train pulled out at 2.30 am and we went via Edinburgh, Berwick, Newcastle (coffee and pies for breakfast), Darlington, Grantham, Essendine (mugs of tea) and Peterborough to Brandon in Suffolk. We were able to exchange words with some of the passengers waiting for trains on the platforms of the stations, and some of the chaps were frantically writing letters telling their folks they were home and hurling them out on the platform asking people if they would post them. Our folks, of course, thought we were still in Italy and it took some time for the Christmas mail to catch up with us.

Pulling into Brandon, the first sight that greeted us was of a land girl canoodling with an Italian prisoner by the level crossing gate; we had picked up sufficient colloquial Italian to shout some remarks that somewhat startled him. On detraining we found the station yard full of TCVs (troop carrying vehicles) ready to take us away. One of the RASC drivers said, 'Have you come here for the battle course?' He narrowly escaped with his life. They drove us some miles out into the wilds to Didlington Camp, near Mundford, consisting of Nissen huts in a copse. By then it was dark and trying to find our way round in the blackout was not easy. I walked straight into a hand-cart which had been left outside a hut with a shaft sticking up in the air and gave myself a black eye.

It was a week before we got off on leave – as usual we were the last in the brigade. Why everyone could not go at once I don't know; presumably there weren't enough trains. We spent most of the time just waiting to go. They gave us a second battledress, which was just as well as we'd been living in our existing one for three months, often in very muddy conditions. The special train took us off on the morning of the 13th. Having been overseas for over two years I was entitled to 21 days leave and had drawn £40 in pay – a fortune in those days. It represented about four month's pay for a sergeant at seven shillings a day (we lost our sixpence a day colonial allowance the day we went on board *Cameronia*; I'm surprised they continued paying it to us in Italy).

There were quite a lot of changes to the scenery in London and on the way out to Malden – holes in the ground where there had once been buildings. Walking home from the station I noticed that there were one or two houses with flags out and in Orchard Avenue there were quite a lot. When I arrived home I enquired what the good news was that had brought all the flags out and was told it was because I was coming home; I was quite flattered. The three weeks were over very quickly, visiting friends and relatives and going to the pictures and to see a number of shows in town. I slept well enough in my bed but found sitting in a chair more difficult after years of sitting on petrol cans. I tended to sit on a stool and prop my book or paper on a chair. Being home gave me a chance to get into a bath again for the first time since I had been in hospital in December 1942, just over a year previously, although we had swum in the Med at Homs. There were one or two air raids and I particularly remember one occasion when my sister and I were visiting our cousin at Raynes Park whose husband was in the Fire Service. When the alarm went, he insisted that we should go on to the roof of their block of flats to see the fun. As there was an ack-ack battery in the park just next to them there was an awful lot of noise and bits of shrapnel were clattering all around. It was a bit too much like home for my peace of mind.

All good things come to an end and by the early hours of Saturday 5 February I was back in camp, thankfully with the weekend in which to settle down. Our first vehicles arrived that morning – Carden-Loyd carriers with which we were to tow the guns. This was disappointing because it was a pre-war design and although slightly bigger than the 'carrier universal' we used in the scout platoon, it was not big enough to carry all the crew and equipment. So we had to have two carriers for every gun, which took an extra driver and brought the risk of being separated in the event of breakdowns, etc. They probably thought that a tracked vehicle would be better across country on the Continent, but we found them difficult to turn round tight corners through farm gates etc. when towing the gun. Moreover, if ambushed on a narrow road it was almost impossible to get the gun into action, as one of our platoons found to its cost. Luckily, whilst we were in Normandy we were able to replace them with American half-tracks which were much better.

A few days later the colonel gave us a lecture in which he told us that the division was to be part of 30 Corps, one of the assault corps in the invasion, news of which was received with some dismay. Whilst overseas we had been getting copies of the English newspapers containing pictures of the vast armies training in Britain for the Second Front, and whilst we did not expect to sit back in England for the rest of the war, it was a bit of a shock to be told we were going to lead the way. After having had two years of it, the troops were quite prepared to let others have their turn. This appears to have been Monty's doing. Despite his claims, I don't believe he really understood his troops. He talked about seeing 'the light of battle in their eyes'; personally, in all my service, I never saw the light of battle in anybody's eyes. He tended to think that the desert war started only when he arrived, forgetting that many of the troops had been at it for a long time before then. Anyway, he brought home the 7th Armoured, 50 Div. and the Highland Div. and a couple of armoured brigades, and they were three of the first four British divisions ashore in Normandy (the fourth being the 3rd Division). I think he lived to regret it because in Normandy he sacked both our divisional commander and brigadier (both very able and popular generals), because the division was 'too sticky' and did not press on as it should. The commander of the Highland Division went the same way because, Monty said, 'The Division did not fight with determination and failed in every operation it had been given to do.' However, its divisional history said 'It contained too many men who had crossed the start line once too often'.

It was said that we were not used to fighting in close country after the desert, but it was not a question of being used to it, but of the consequence of fighting in it. In the desert armoured formations advanced in line abreast on a broad front and more often than not the enemy could be seen when still out of range. When action was joined, each tank had a more or less equal chance with those to left and right of it. In Europe on the other hand, the advance, more often than not, was along a single road and the first warning of the enemy was almost certainly a direct hit on the leading vehicle, be it tank, armoured car or carrier. The crew, particularly if they had previously baled out of burning vehicles several times, were therefore very cautious and would often creep forward on foot at every bend to make sure the coast was clear. If opposition was sighted, they would be equally cautious in manoeuvring round the flanks to force them out. This was compounded by the continued superiority of the German tanks. Our armoured units were re-equipped with Cromwell tanks when they got back to England. One of the crews asked a delivery driver what they were like. He launched into a dissertation on its virtues, only to be interrupted with 'No, no, how many escape hatches does it have?' In fact, I believe they did have an extra one cut. A 'green' formation would be much more likely to press on regardless, and the higher command were quite prepared to accept the loss of a few tank or carrier crews to keep the advance going. But the chaps in the front had only one life to lose and when the airwaves started turning blue with exhortations to press on the unspoken response was 'Come past if you want, mate, I'm not stopping you.' Men have only a finite amount of courage which gradually gets used up, and the only way out, as the saying goes, was 'on a stretcher or six feet under'. I was surprised that so few of our chaps deserted before we went to Normandy. I think there were about four in our platoon, and one of them wrote me a letter of apology, but I believe that in one brigade of 50 Div. there were over a thousand on the run at one time.

But this is anticipating events. We spent the next three months at Mundford mostly collecting guns, vehicles and equipment and getting them ready, firing the guns on Hunstanton ranges and small arms at Swaffham and Thetford. There was one two-day exercise with the tanks in the Stanford battle area, and we did quite a lot of assault boating, rafting, etc. (none of which we ever had to put into practice). On one occasion we succeeded in tipping the gun over into the water, which did it no good at all. One of our carriers provided a surprise for a family living on the road to Hunstanton when it came through their front window as they were sitting down to breakfast, but luckily there were no personal injuries. We were inspected by Monty and by the King (always a bad sign) and had a lecture from the divisional commander. I got home for seven days leave at the beginning of March and also had two 48-hour passes. There were still a few air raids going on but the nearest bombs to home fell in Worcester Park. In camp we used to go to the pictures in Brandon or to the 'Desert Rat Theatre' where there were occasional ENSA concerts, or spend the evening in the Salvation Army canteen.

On 9 May we moved to our concentration area – Camp S5J at Brentwood in Essex. Here we got down to waterproofing the carriers, which involved stripping down the engine and putting sealing compound over the electrical parts which would be damaged by water and fixing pipes to extend the exhausts and air intakes upwards, hopefully above the waterline. We were supposed to be able to go through four feet of water. My driver had a series of visits to the dentist, so I had to do a lot of the waterproofing myself which worried me a bit (it worried me even more later). It was only the engine that was waterproofed, the carrier itself filled with water so we had to be careful where we put our personal kit. This took about a week, then we had a few days loading the carriers with all the equipment and having a few lectures (e.g. how to escape from a prison camp). I managed a 36-hour leave before the camp was sealed on 26 May. It was surrounded by barbed wire and was guarded by Bluecaps, a sort of second-class military police who had not left England and were unlikely to do so. This caused a certain amount of resentment and it became a point of honour to go out through the wire. One day all the battalion's sergeants were summoned by the colonel. He had been driving away from the camp in his staff car and had passed numbers of the battalion coming up the hill back to camp, including some sergeants. He said, 'I have nothing to say about being out of camp, but I will not have sergeants of the battalion not saluting the colonel when he passes in his car.' The colonel was very well liked – he had a cleft palate and therefore a slight speech impediment and was known as Nuff-nuff or Uncle Nuffers.

Three days later we marshalled ourselves in 'ship serials' – the units were all split up, so that the sinking of one ship would not mean the loss of a complete unit. I went with I Company with my two guns and three carriers, the fourth being left behind to reduce the call on shipping requirements for the first lift. On Whit Monday, 29 May, we set off for Tilbury to load the vehicles on the ship. My driver had nipped home on the Sunday and been picked up by the Redcaps and incarcerated instead of being reported and sent back to us. As a result I had to drive the carrier to the docks myself (and drive it ashore on the beaches – not with a great deal of confidence). Although it is only about twelve miles from Brentwood to Tilbury, and we left at midday, we spent the night on marshalling stands on the Southend Road and hung about there all the next day, not moving down to Tilbury until 7 pm. There we carried out the final stages of waterproofing, after which the vehicles could only be driven a short distance. Next morning we waited for the dockers to arrive and start the loading. They were supposed to start at 8 am but by half past only a few of them had turned up and were gloomily surveying the vehicles and the ship (an American Liberty ship called *Charles W. Eliot*), trying out the winches and getting the slings ready. Then a mobile canteen came driving up, and as we surged forward they said 'Sorry, dockers only,' which improved our tempers no end. After half an hour or so they got to work, but by the time they knocked off for lunch at midday only a handful of vehicles were aboard and we began to think they'd have to postpone D-Day. They moved a bit faster in the afternoon and eventually all the vehicles were aboard and we were driven back to camp. Two days later we moved down the road to Warley Barracks where we stayed the night and changed our money into Francs – the first official indication that we were going to land in France. Next day, Sunday, 4 June, we left the barracks at 5.30 pm and were taken to Tilbury, where we boarded the *Charles W. Eliot* in mid-stream, moving down next morning to anchor off Southend with the rest of the convoy. The next day was D-Day. We remained at anchor all that day as a result of the 24-hour postponement and got under way at six next morning. Personally, I was not optimistic of my chances of returning in one piece, having survived two years in the desert and Italy. It seemed a bit much to think that my luck would hold during the much more difficult campaign that was likely to lie ahead.

Normandy

❦

Leaving the Thames estuary, we passed through the Dover Straits at mid-morning and were shelled by the German guns at Cap Gris-Nez, which we found disconcerting as it wasn't possible to dig a slit trench on the deck of a ship. One ship was hit but our own guns opened up in reply and a couple of MLs came out of Dover and laid a smokescreen. For food we had a copper of hot water on the deck; we put tins of meat and veg in to heat them up and then used the hot water remaining to make tea. We had a few cans of self-heating soup for when we got ashore – you just pulled a tag and they heated up; it worked quite well.

We arrived off the beach at 10 am on the 8th. It was quiet in our sector ('Gold' sector), the shelling being some way inland, but most of the LCTs seemed to be stranded on the beach ('Jig' beach – east of Arromanches). There was little movement in the area apart from warships bombarding and we were unable to get ashore until next day. Unloading started at 7 am but it was 4 pm before our turn came. It was a somewhat alarming experience, as we had to climb down the scramble netting to the LCT and then stand and guide the carriers and guns whilst they were lowered to the deck. As the LCT was rising and falling about six feet alongside the ship it was a bit tricky. We eventually got going and landed on Jig beach about 6 pm. My carrier was the second ashore. A Jeep went first and promptly 'drowned' just off the ramp, which bothered me, because a carrier steers by its brakes (to turn left, you brake the left track, and so on), and when the brakes get wet they don't work, so I was afraid that when I got round the Jeep I would not be able to straighten up again. But all went well despite being up to my knees in water and once we were on dry land a few smart applications of the brakes got them dried out and working again. We drove off the beach through the gaps in the minefields to the battalion concentration area at Sommervieu, about three miles E-N-E of Bayeux, where we started getting as much of the de-proofing done as possible whilst the light remained, interrupted by a flying visit from a few Me's. The Luftwaffe also came over to disturb our sleep. Next day we finished de-proofing and sorting ourselves out. Two of our companies were already in action and suffering casualties on the road to Tilly-sur-Seulles but the long wait off the beaches had put us behind. The motor companies were without their carriers – through an 'administrative error' the ship carrying them was diverted to Cowes, where it remained at anchor for five days. Next day, Sunday, we moved through Bayeux and down the road as far as Blary, where my other carrier caught up with us from the rear party.

June 1944

I am sorry I haven't been able to write sooner but we've had rather a lot to do lately, with not much spare time. I'm also very sorry I wasn't able to get home again before we left but we were somewhat hemmed in towards the end. Anyway, we're settling down a bit over here now, and getting used to being on the move again.

We had an entirely uneventful trip across and as we beetled ashore, a bottle of Scotch in one hand and a French dictionary in the other, I felt rather a cross between William the Conqueror and a Cook's tourist.

I am sorry to hear about the raids on England with pilotless planes, I hope they haven't been troubling you much.

So far we have had one lot of papers from home, but as I have a wireless on my carrier now, we are able to get the news on the short wave if we are not too busy.

Having passed through 50 Div. who had made the initial landing and captured Bayeux, which was undamaged, our brigade was supposed to move south through Tilly-sur-Seulles, Villers Bocage and Aunay-sur-Odon to capture the high ground round Mont Pinçon. Monty's plan was that it should be captured a few days after D-Day, but in fact it took two months. The country is unsuitable for tanks because of the small fields with big hedges (the Bocage) and woods. 131 Brigade (the Queens) were only just landing and our motor

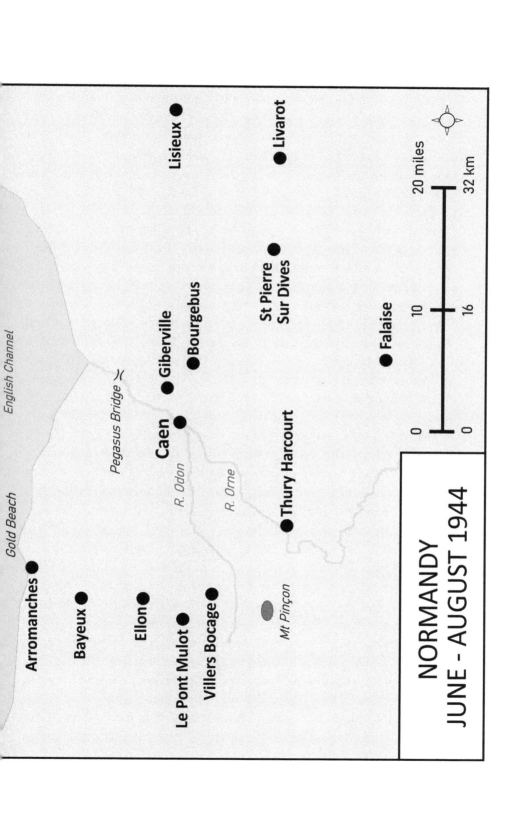

NORMANDY
JUNE - AUGUST 1944

companies were too few in numbers to clear the villages and stop the Germans from filtering back into them, so progress was slow. The Americans on our right were meeting virtually no opposition so it was decided to disengage from the front and make a right hook, using the side roads on the boundary with the Americans so as to approach Villers Bocage from the west. We set off at 4 pm on 12 June, leaguering for the night at the hamlet of La Hulotière, near Livry.

Next morning we got on to the Caumont – Villers Bocage road but after a while came to a prolonged halt, the loud noises ahead indicating that the front of the column had run into trouble. The CLY were the leading armoured regiment, with our A Company and the anti-tank guns of 6 Platoon from our company under their command. They motored down the road and into Villers Bocage without opposition and were greeted by a cheering crowd of French people. The leading squadron drove straight through to occupy the high ground about one mile to the east on the road to Caen. A Company and 6 Platoon followed on, but remained on the road for the time being; they were urged to close up nose to tail so that the following squadron of tanks could get into the village to protect the crossroads. The colonel of the CLY went forward to the high ground to reconnoitre the position, as did all the officers of A Company, to pick out their positions before calling their platoons forward. Suddenly a Tiger tank emerged from the woods to the south of the road. The Tiger was a real monster with an 88 mm gun and frontal armour too thick to be penetrated by our tank and anti-tank guns even at point-blank range. He picked off the two rear tanks of the leading squadron, then drove down the hedge beside the road blowing up A Company's half-tracks and 6 Platoon's carriers one by one until he reached the centre of the village. There he disposed of four more tanks of the CLY before turning back to rejoin his companions. Everything was chaos. The road was completely blocked with burning vehicles. The infantry, in a state of uncertainty because all of their officers had gone forward, had no answer to the Tiger with only their small arms. One of the sergeants in 6 Platoon, 'Donkey' Bray, managed to get his 6-pounder unhooked and into action and claimed to have hit an armoured car and a couple of half-tracks, but when his shots started bouncing off an approaching Tiger at point-blank range he decided that discretion was the better part of valour.

A battalion of the Queens came up to defend the village where quite a fierce little battle developed before the Germans were thrown out, but no one could reach the squadron on the high ground and their tanks were knocked out and the survivors, together with those of A Company, were taken prisoner. The CLY had 27 tanks knocked out and lost fourteen officers and 86 men. A Company lost 80, including three officers killed. About 30 of them and about half of 6 Platoon got back but Roger Butler, the platoon commander, was killed. One of their sergeants, Jock Callan, we saw again right at the end of the war when we liberated the POW camp at Fallingbostel where he had been incarcerated – he was a lot thinner by then. Several of the others got back earlier as they were still in Rennes when the Yanks arrived.

Meanwhile we had hastily taken up defensive positions near Amayé, a couple of miles west of Villers Bocage. The position was somewhat dicey, as the road back for several miles ran through German territory. To the north the Panzer Lehr Division were where we had expected them, but to the south the 2nd Panzer Division had arrived undetected from beyond the Seine, as had the two companies of Tiger tanks which had caused the initial chaos. From time to time they were able to cut the road behind us. In the close bocage country it was difficult to see what was happening. There was a tank gun firing so close to us that it seemed to be in the next field, so I gingerly moved forward to have a look but after crossing two fields I could still see nothing. It still seemed very close but I decided it was not an immediate threat and beat a retreat. In the early evening the troops and tanks still in Villers withdrew to our perimeter and we spent a somewhat restless night. Next day we were under continuous shellfire and the position was so crowded that a number of vehicles were hit. One shell landed close to our gun pit and wounded two of my section; one of them was crouching shoulder to shoulder with me and a piece of shrapnel hit him in the arm that was touching mine – a cushy one really. The other lad was badly hit in the stomach and died in hospital later; he had only joined us a few days before and I hardly knew his name. During the afternoon the 2nd Panzer launched several attacks, one against the Queens and one against I Company, who had two officers killed as well as their sergeant major and a sergeant, George Walley, who had been in our company in the desert. These attacks were broken up by our RHA battery firing over open sights, and by a considerable barrage from the American gunners who had a liaison officer, a captain, with us. He said he expected to be court-martialled when he got back to them because he had ordered a 'serenade', which meant rapid fire by all guns within range, and only a general had authority to give this order. We had a similar thing called a Victor target; it was quite something and I wouldn't have liked to be on the receiving end.

That night we pulled back, covered by a 100-bomber raid on Villers to create a diversion and drown the noise of our vehicles, through Briquessard to La Mulotiere, where we sorted ourselves out and tried to catch up on some sleep, having had little for three nights. My section was then roused and sent off with a section of carriers to block a river crossing, involving more digging in, and returning to the platoon the following morning. The action at Villers has been the subject of considerable controversy ever since, because if we had maintained our hold there the campaign in the bridgehead might have been materially shortened. The division was unfairly blamed and the divisional commander and brigadier eventually sacked, whereas the blame really lay with the corps commander. The close country soaked up infantry like a sponge and the Queens Brigade and ourselves did not have sufficient numbers to hold our position and keep open a five-mile line of communication against attacks from both sides by two panzer divisions. The divisional commander asked for another infantry brigade, failing which he would have to pull back after 24 hours. The corps commander refused, believing that 50 Div. attacking south from Tilly would relieve the pressure, but their attack got nowhere, so we pulled back. The corps commander had also held back our right hook for 24 hours, otherwise we would have been well-established beyond Villers before the 2nd Panzers and the Tigers arrived. The CLY and A Company could be blamed for not having some sort of flank protection out, but they took a chance on a brief stop and got caught – half an hour either way and they would not have been caught in an impossible position.

After one day's rest we moved to take up positions at Le Pont Mulot, but our carrier got stuck in the mud during the dark and we did not get into position until next morning. Having dug in, we had to move again at last light and dig in once more when we arrived.

June 1944

You will notice the new address with this letter, I understand it means 'British West European Forces' but probably you know for sure better than I do.

The weather has been a bit better the last two days and we are indulging in a spot of sun bathing at the moment. When it gets too hot we retire under the shade of a pear tree. We are in an orchard and even our tarpaulin tent is disguised to look like a Cox's Orange Pippin! A wonderful thing is camouflage.

We haven't had a lot to do with the local population so far, but they don't seem particularly keen on being 'liberated' – it seems to be rather a case of 'mes amis, les Allemands'. I'd sooner have the Iti's any time. They certainly are not the least bit hungry and they are pretty well-dressed, especially for a country district like this – all the latest fashions, silk stockings etc.

Well, things have gone pretty well for the first three weeks anyway, of course the big push has yet to come, but it looks as if the Yanks have got Cherbourg pretty well wrapped up now. I only hope the docks haven't been knocked about too much. By the way, I noticed there was rather a lot of boloney about us in the papers on the 18th and 19th – don't take too much notice of that. I think the correspondents must have been imagining things a bit.

They seem to be going flat out in Italy now, they certainly made a good job of it this time. It will have a big effect on this campaign too, as we have already found out.

I hope these flying bombs haven't been bothering you much, they must be rather nasty. Over here all we see is an endless procession of Spitfires, Typhoons, Mustangs, Thunderbolts, Marauders and all the rest of the bunch – all day and night they seem to be going over.

We stayed for ten days, holding about a mile and a half of front, with occasional shelling and patrol activity on both sides which cost a few casualties. One young rifleman was lucky one morning when dawn stand-to was over and everyone had returned to sleep. He was on sentry dozing with his blanket draped around his shoulders when he heard a sound, looked up and found a six-foot panzer grenadier immediately in front of him pointing his Schmeisser at him. The lad promptly pulled the blanket over his head and screamed. The German just pinched his rifle and sloped off – why he didn't shoot him I don't know; perhaps he had got lost and was only interested in getting home. One night B Echelon, some miles back where A Company was re-forming, was shelled and three officers were among the killed and another ex- B Company sergeant, Alf Reeves, was wounded. By now the battalion had lost fourteen officers and 165 men in the two weeks we had been ashore; not a very good start. The division had lost 1,149.

Visiting the graves of fallen comrades – Bayeux War Cemetery, 1991

At last light on 28 June we were relieved by the Gloucesters and moved back to La Bigne, north of St Honorine de Ducy, where we were able to lie in and catch up on some sleep. Being midsummer the nights were short and what with stand-to and guards, sleeping time was at a premium. Otherwise we were camouflaging and weapon-cleaning. After 48 hours we moved again to a field at Ellon, between Bayeux and Jerusalem, where we went into Corps Reserve and had just over a fortnight's rest. As usual, once we had camouflaged ourselves under the trees we were busy cleaning the guns and the vehicles and had a daily ration of gun drill, with a few lectures and other activities. There was a lot of rain which kept everything somewhat muddy. Mail had been coming over regularly, but it couldn't have been so quick the other way. It was not until 8 July that I heard they had received the first letter I had sent home after landing. Amongst the first mail I received after landing in Normandy was an income tax return for 1943/44 from the Inland Revenue! Unfortunately, it was destroyed by enemy action! Whilst in the back areas we were able to augment our rations with fresh milk, butter, cream, camembert cheese and the local firewater, Calvados. After the first sampling, I tended to avoid the latter, preferring the occasional bottle of Scotch which, as a sergeant, I was allowed. We even started getting some fresh bread. Cigarettes, however, were still in short supply.

On 17 July we moved a few miles east to join 8 Corps for Operation Goodwood, the attack southeast of Caen by all three armoured divisions. The following morning we joined the enormous traffic jam and clouds of dust waiting to get across the River Orne and through the minefields beyond. Pegasus Bridge had been augmented by five Bailey bridges but the three armoured divisions had over 8,000 vehicles to get across. Luckily the RAF had control of the air (their fighters raised enormous clouds of dust taking off from the airstrips in the bridgehead) and the Luftwaffe was unable to take advantage of the opportunity, having to confine its activities mainly to night bombing, although their fighters did make an occasional swift dash across the lines. We eventually got across the river as far as Cuverville, where we spent the night. The battle had not gone well, despite a colossal preliminary bombardment by Bomber Command. The German tanks and anti-tank guns seemed to have survived this, at least in sufficient numbers to give the 11th Armoured Div. (which included my old battalion of the LRB, now the 8th Rifle Brigade) a very sticky time, losing two-thirds of their tanks. It took so long to get clear of the congestion that it was late afternoon before our tanks could get up to support them. Next morning we moved on across the Caen – Troarn railway south of Giberville, where we sat down for nearly six days in a growing sea of mud.

July 1944

Well, the news seems to get brighter and brighter – we've just heard of Hitler's narrow squeak – what a pity! Still, it may be the writing on the wall. I hope they stir things up a bit in Germany, anyway. Of course, you have heard by now of the push SE of Caen, which has gone off quite well, while the Russians still seem to be making a lot of headway.

We are still getting bread – about a slice and a half every other day. You also asked about breakfast: we have either sausages or bacon, usually sausages, which bear a faint resemblance to the peacetime article.

The mud is getting muddier – if this is summer I hope we're not here in winter!

Meanwhile our motor companies and the tanks tried unsuccessfully to winkle the Germans out of their defensive positions on the Bourgebus ridge, with occasional bouts of shelling during which the company's carriers were hit and several people wounded, including Norman Griffiths. One of the vehicles caught fire but we managed to get the ammunition off to avoid the firework display that would otherwise have occurred. The Luftwaffe also came along at night to disturb our sleep. There were so many vehicles parked in the congested area east of the Orne that hits were inevitable, particularly as the whole area was overlooked by German OPs. With no progress being made on our front, the Canadians continued attacking on our right, southwards from Caen, and on the evening of the 28th we moved round through Caen, or what remained of it, to the village of Ifs. Next morning our tanks went forward to support the Canadians but the attack did not get very far. It was a very unpleasant area and we were shelled and mortared throughout most of the next five days, with a bit of night bombing thrown in. One morning I woke up to find the body of a German airman two or three yards from my slit trench (which was the safest place to sleep). One of their bombers had been shot down and he had bailed out but his parachute had not opened. The material was divided up and later sent home to wives and girlfriends when leave started. With all the racket going on I hadn't heard the thump when he landed. At the end of the first day the section commanders were waiting beside the platoon commander's carrier for him to return with orders about going into the leaguer with the tanks. When he got back he just said 'Follow me', but my section was furthest away, round a spur, and by the time I had run back, got them started up and re-emerged, the rest of the platoon had vanished. There were vehicles going in all directions – unlike the bocage, the area was open rolling country, largely cornfields heavily populated by May bugs, and therefore we were not confined to the roads. After fruitlessly chasing several groups of vehicles in the gathering gloom, I decided to call a halt and we stopped where we were before one of the carriers or guns fell into a slit trench. Next morning we moved back to our previous position and rejoined our platoon. We moved again a short distance, getting bogged down on the way, and spent half the night digging in, luckily, because we were shelled all the next day. One of our chaps was wounded and Dicky Dyer, one of the remaining members of the old Farnham crowd, died of the wounds he had received the previous day. Two days later, 29 July, we pulled out and thankfully moved back to our old field at Ellon near Bayeux for a rest, where one of my chaps promptly shot himself in the foot with his Sten – I still don't know if it was an accident or not. There we exchanged our carriers for American White half-tracks, more powerful vehicles which were roomier and more comfortable for the crew.

We had only two days in which to make the switch before moving forward again, this time to our old stamping ground north of Villers Bocage, through La Belle Epine and Torteval to Cantaloup, gradually moving southeast in the direction of Thury-Harcourt. After twelve days of this with nothing more alarming than a spot of night bombing, and one occasion when I had to clear a lot of mines from the position where I wanted to put my gun, we had a minor shock. Our motor companies were having a sticky time, as were the Queens, trying to push forward in the thick and hilly country. The three Queens Battalions had 1,000 casualties in three weeks – the 5th and 6th were down to a strength of only one company each and the 7th were not much better. The flow of reinforcements from home was negligible at this time; they had to disband a complete infantry division (the 59th) to help make up the strength of the rest. They also disbanded several armoured brigades in order to make up the strength of the others. Apart from the general shortage of manpower and the 300,000 plus casualties already sustained by the army since the war started, the problem was compounded by the bright sparks at the War Office (Head Office, as our colonel used to call it) failing to realise that it was the infantry who sustained most of the casualties. By the end of July, over 70% of the casualties in Normandy had been sustained by the infantry, but only 15% of the available reinforcements were infantrymen. Because our motor companies were so short we were greeted on 11 August with the news that the number of anti-tank guns in our company was to be cut from twelve to six and the crews of the other six, including myself, would be available to reinforce them.

8 August 1944

I am feeling a bit browned off at the moment, they have shifted Charlie to another platoon, much to his disgust – he wanted to revert to rifleman but they threatened to send him to another company, so he's got to put up with it. There are only two of us left in the platoon out of those who went out to Egypt – the others are scattered all over the place now. They don't seem to realise what it means to be shifted out of a platoon you've been in for four years, as Charlie has. I hope they don't try to do it to me, or there will be a bust up!

A couple of days later, on my 23rd birthday, I was given a reprieve when I was put in charge of the six surplus guns, which I took back to B Echelon. There I was given a party of spare tank crews and told to train them up to man the guns and use them for the protection of B Echelon. The tankies were very suspicious of this; most of them had baled out of tanks several times and were pretty bomb-happy. They were convinced that, once trained, we would no longer stay with B Echelon but be sent forward to the front line. I told them that if they were so scared of anti-tank guns when in tanks, they ought to be happy to man anti-tank guns, but they didn't agree; however we got along. There were about 30 of them and I was the only NCO.

August 1944

Thank you for all your birthday wishes, I've had quite a lot of mail lately. Yesterday, to celebrate my birthday, they decided to have a bit of a sort-out and swap round, whereby I've now temporarily got an absolutely fantastic but cushy job in B Echelon, which of course is well back. I was being chipped all day yesterday and greeted by such remarks as 'Base Wallah' etc. Still, to make up for it, they give me plenty to worry about. I've about 30 men and fourteen vehicles to be responsible for, and no other NCOs. Still, San Fairy Ann!

I hope the buzz bombs aren't giving you too much trouble these days – the sooner we can push Jerry out of Northern France and Holland the better. Things seem to be going pretty well now – he has only got a very small escape gap left, and the Air Force are giving him a pretty good pounding, day and night. Anyway, everything seems to be pretty rosy.

After three days we moved east to the Canadian Army sector, to St Aignan de Cramesnil, south of Garcelles Secqueville, southeast of Caen. The division was to advance from St Pierre sur Dives to Livarot and Lisieux, and we moved forward with B Echelon to a spot west of St Pierre whilst the Queens secured a bridgehead over the River Vie at Livarot. The 5th Tanks with I Company and one of our platoons rushed forward and 'bounced' the bridge at Fervaques. They had a good time at first, as the Germans were still bowling up and down the road, but when they realised what had happened they reacted violently and we had a number of casualties, including my old friend Charlie Parker who was wounded in the leg (and I think left with a permanent limp), and three of his platoon's half-tracks were knocked out. They were more or less cut off for two days before the area could be cleared. We then moved forward to Marolles, east of Lisieux, and on to the north of Giverville as the division moved forward to the River Risle at Pont Authon and thence towards the Seine. Then they had a couple of days rest before embarking on a dash through northern France with Ghent, 220 miles away, as the objective.

The night before, I was roused from bed at 11 pm to dash back to the platoon as they were short of a section commander. I never did find out what happened to my 30 tankies; there were no other NCOs with me.

Across Northern France

I got no sleep that night because we started off at 3.30 am through Louviers (going in the ditch on the way) and across the Seine at St Pierre, through Gournay and carrying on all night northward to Aumale. Here we got stuck for the rest of the day as the Canadian Armoured Div. had got on to our centre line. Everyone was trying to get across the Somme and as the only bridge in our sector collapsed after one squadron of tanks had got across, we were eventually allowed to use one just west of Amiens which 'belonged' to another corps. Now we really started motoring. The objective for the day was St Pol, some 70 miles away. The Germans on the Normandy front had disintegrated and were putting up little resistance; we kept coming across small parties who were generally only too glad to give themselves up – they were safer with us than at the mercy of the French population. However, the Germany Army in the Pas de Calais was intact and they had sent forces in some strength to places like Auxi-le-Chateau, St Pol, Lillers, Béthune and La Bassée, all of which were on our centre line. We soon ran out of maps, except odd road maps people had been able to scrounge, which made things a bit difficult, and we had to rely on signposts and the French people. The farther we went the more excited the people seemed to be. We were showered with fruit and wine, Union Jacks appeared by magic and everywhere we were entertained by *Tipperary* and *Pack up Your Troubles*, which they all seemed to know. For some reason we were always greeted with 'Goodbye, Tommy', although I don't think they meant it. It gave us great pleasure to go past several buzz-bomb sites and to know that they would no longer be used on London (We hadn't heard of the V2 rockets by then).

September 1944

Just a short note while I've got the chance, as we have stopped for a while.

At the moment I'm back with the platoon and we are having a terrific time. I haven't been to sleep for four nights so far – we can't catch Jerry up 'no how', except for stragglers. Every time we stop, we go and have a look in the nearest wood and guarantee to find at least two Jerries sleeping in a hole somewhere – dead beat.

The French are all over us up here and doing a lot of good work themselves. We caught our first 'buzz-bomb' base this morning – absolutely smothered with bomb craters.

They seem to be moving like lightning now – we look like being in Belgium any moment, and Holland too. It looks as if Jerry intends to try and make a last stand on the frontier somewhere. The 8th Army has broken through the Gothic line too, so they will soon be knocking at the Brenner.

By the way, I saw my first 'Doodle Bug' today – it went doodling overhead in the early hours, and went off with a 'womph' somewhere miles back.

Well, we are just on the move again. We'll give 'em 'buzz bombs'!

P.S. The people have been showing us souvenirs given them by the troops in '40 and '14.

Later. We have just stopped for a few minutes on the road again – more people waving and shouting, more homemade Union Jacks, more vin blanc and vin rouge, and of course several tired Jerries. We got quite a lot of Jerry sweets. We were thinking of sending some home, but they are not much cop so we have been chucking them to the kids instead; they are highly delighted.

We have just passed another Flying Bomb site – one more less! Sorry you have had so many 'Doodles' lately, but we are fixing them up fairly fast now. We are still having an amazing time, being swamped with apples, pears, plums, vin blanc, vin rouge, cognac, beer and coffee (ersatz).

We set out at 7 am on 2 September, crossing the Somme just west of Amiens and then on through Doullens, by-passing St Pol where there was a strong force of Germans which we left to the 5th Queens. We carried on through the night as far as Cauchy, five miles south of Lillers, which we reached at four in the morning, and then had to dig in. There were many Germans about and they had closed in behind us. We (our battalion and the 1st Tanks) were in fact cut off from the rest of the division, most of whom were around St Pol. The division was in action along eighteen miles of road, which was also our centre line, with some of the Queens still trying to clear the Germans out of Frévent; this made the supply of petrol etc. difficult. 1st Tanks and C Company went forward to clear Lillers – there was a certain amount of street fighting and they had some casualties. In the afternoon we were ordered off again, to Hinges on the La Bassée Canal north of Béthune. Going through Lillers we had the biggest welcome yet, but this was brought to a sudden stop. Jerry was following us up the road; my half-track was the last in the column and we were going along slowly in fits and starts when a Frenchman on a bicycle came pedalling furiously up behind us and shot past shouting 'Chars Bosches'. In an instant the people disappeared, the flags were hauled in and windows slammed. I kept a nervous eye back down the road, but the Germans never caught up with us. We were somewhat concerned at leaving Lillers unprotected but had orders to press on to the Aire Canal, still aiming for Ghent. The following divisions were still a long way back – there were limits to the number of units they could maintain in the advance as we rapidly increased the distance from the bridgehead. The Germans did try to get back into Lillers but the Resistance were well enough organised to retain control of the centre of the town, although I believe some civilians were killed on the outskirts.

The Resistance forces were a great help to us at this time. We called them the Maquis, although this was not strictly accurate. They provided information as to the whereabouts of groups of Germans, acted as guides and so on. A number of them 'joined up' and stayed with us for the rest of the war – seventeen of them from this area (two of them were killed later). At first they were dressed in civvies, then they were given old battle dress blouses until we stopped for a few days' rest somewhere and the colonel and RSM were horrified to see these scruffy figures 'on parade', whereupon they were properly fitted out with uniform. At first they were given money from regimental funds but eventually they were paid by the French, who had tried and failed to persuade them to go into the French Army. One of them was named Noel Paniez; the troops called him Christmas Basket. Later we collected some Belgians as well. We had one, Paul Gois, who was eventually made a sergeant; after he had gone home, I met him in Brussels whilst I was on a 48 hours' leave. After the war I met him in England a couple of times and on one occasion we visited the regimental museum. He was always very proud of his association with the regiment and when he died in 1999 the official notice of his death called him 'Paul Gois, Ingenieur Commercial SOLVAY, attached to 1st Battalion, The Rifle Brigade'. To see these Frenchmen and Belgians interrogating Germans was quite something – they really hated them

Comrades relaxing – Paul Gois second left. (Ken Phillips Collection)

– but we had a German Jew in our company who was even worse. He need not have been with us, because if he had been taken prisoner he would have come to a sticky end, but he volunteered as he wanted to get his own back. To digress, we captured four young Jerries about this time from an SS Division. They were only about seventeen and three of them were scared stiff, but the other one was a real cocky little Nazi. So we took him away from the others, gave him a shovel and made him start digging, after taking suitable measurements. As it gradually dawned on him that he was digging his own grave all his bluster disappeared, and when he finally collapsed in tears we let him rejoin the other three.

Meanwhile we moved on to Hinges, on the Aire Canal north of Béthune, where we took up positions protecting the bridge whilst the leading elements pushed on through Locon to Estaires, only to have the bridge over the Lys blown in their faces, so they were called back to Béthune. There was not enough bridging equipment to cope with all the canals and rivers and the divisional commander was trying to get permission to shift a bit further east. Before getting back, however, this column found itself with Germans on three sides, and the RHA battery was firing with half its guns facing north and the other half south. It was that sort of war at this time.

Belgium and the Netherlands

❦

The next day, the 4th, we were waiting for the Welsh Division to come up and relieve us on the canal, and also for petrol. A small force of two armoured regiments plus A Company was sent off on a dash for Ghent, which they reached next day. We were eventually relieved at 3 am on the 5th and moved through Béthune to Mazingarbe, on the Lens road, where we stopped for three days, finding a church hall in which to make ourselves comfortable whilst they were still trying to clear up the centre line behind us. The people here were just as enthusiastic, but were clearly much more short of food than in the farming districts of Normandy; they seemed to live mainly on potatoes, tomatoes and fruit. We left Mazingarbe at midday on the 8th, crossed into Belgium and drove through Tournai, Ronse (Renaix) and Oudenarde to Oombergen, southeast of Ghent. The Belgians gave us an even bigger welcome than the French. We spent the evening with a family in their home in which we were also able to spend the night, drinking and singing songs, English and Flemish alternately, and listening to their tales of the Moffe, as they called the Germans. One song I remember was about the various band instruments with everyone going through the motions of playing each instrument in turn. Another was making fun of the Moffe, but I never got it translated from the Flemish. The relief of the people in Northern France and Belgium at being 'liberated' was such that one could have no doubts as to whether what we were doing was worthwhile. They were quite prepared to accept the damage and casualties caused by bombing and shelling, even if it came from us, so long as it got the Germans off their backs. We had very little sleep for ten days but the exhilaration kept us going.

The following morning we pressed on through Wetteren to Lokeren, where we were protecting a bridge over the Scheldt, shifting the following day to Waasmunster, near Hamme, and then to the north of St Niklaas. After a couple of days we moved on, but the day we moved, 12 September, I was appointed platoon sergeant, so had to make a rapid transfer to the PHQ (Platoon Headquarters) half-track with just myself and the driver (the platoon commander had a carrier, with a driver/batman and wireless operator). The job meant dealing with all the administration including rations, clothing and equipment, being responsible for discipline, detailing men for guards, fatigues, etc., and generally helping the platoon commander and standing in for him in his absence. Apart from personal kit, each section had in the region of 125 different items of equipment in varying quantities and PHQ had nearly as many. Keeping check on all these and their serviceability often became a time-consuming activity when we were supposed to be having a rest. That night we went through Hamme and Dendermonde to Sint-Katelijne-Waver, north of Mechelen where we had three days' rest before moving to the Albert Canal between Herentals and Geel, east of Antwerp. Here the platoon commander and I went for a recce along the canal bank and were wondering how we could stick our heads up over the dyke, which was along our side of the canal, without being spotted by the Jerries just a few yards away across the canal. As it happened the RAF obliged us by flying over and distracting them, so we were able to have a good shufti including pinpointing the positions from which they were firing light ack-ack.

Next day was the day of the airborne landings at Arnhem, Nijmegen and Eindhoven, and the sky was full of transport planes and gliders and their fighter escorts, met by a barrage of flak from the German positions. A couple of days later a standing patrol of C Company on the canal bank to our left was caught napping by a party of Germans who had got across on a wrecked bridge. Their corporal was killed and although the rest got away they left some weapons behind, so we took out a patrol that night to recover the body and the weapons. We were a bit concerned that the Germans might have left booby-traps, but it passed off without incident. Months later, I was coming home on leave in the train to Antwerp when I looked out of the window and found we were just passing through Herentals and over the (rebuilt)

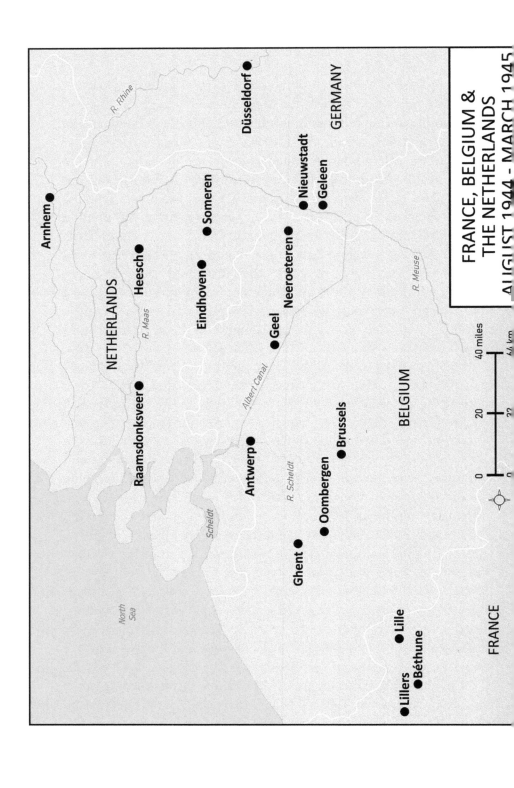

FRANCE, BELGIUM &
THE NETHERLANDS
AUGUST 1944 - MARCH 1945

bridge near which were the slit trenches where the incident had occurred; it seemed strange to see it again in a peaceful setting.

After five days we moved across the Albert Canal into the bridgehead at Geel, on through Mol and up to the canal just north of it. Once again we left our 6-pounders behind and acted as infantry. There was a row of houses along the road leading to a wrecked bridge over the canal and the Germans were on the far bank. In particular there was a sniper in a house by the bridge bank who made himself a nuisance every time we showed ourselves. There was an OP there too, so we were constantly being shelled and mortared. I got on to Company HQ and asked if the gunners could do anything about it. In due course they said they could but hadn't an OP to spare so would I please spot the fall of shot myself. I wasn't too keen on this, as it meant going up to the attic and peering through a hole in the roof of our house, which was only about 60 yards from the target. In due course they fired a ranging shot – straight into the house behind me. I hastily said 'Up one hundred' and they soon managed to put some rounds into the house whereupon the sniper nipped away smartly and we weren't bothered any more. That night a Jerry patrol came across the canal and crept up the street towards our position. We were ready and waiting but for some reason they turned back before they got close enough for us to see them. Twenty-four hours later they had all gone. It was all quiet at dawn stand-to, and about an hour later we saw a woman and two girls picking their way down to the far bank waving Belgian flags. We clambered over the bridge to meet them and they told us the Moffe had gone in the night. Our platoon commander borrowed a couple of bicycles and, taking one of the chaps with him, cycled four miles up the road to Retie where, with the help of the locals, he made a series of telephone calls around the area to find out where the Germans were and where they were not.

Meanwhile the Arnhem operation was not going well. It was some 60 miles north of the bridgehead and although the Guards Armoured Div. had been able to break out and join up with the American paratroops at Eindhoven, and thence advance up the road to Nijmegen, they could not break through the last few miles to

Arnhem. The country was largely flooded. The tanks had to stick to the main road, which was raised on an embankment, and as each tank came along the Germans couldn't miss knocking them out. The 'front' from Eindhoven was little more than the width of the road, and the supply line was constantly being cut by German attacks from both sides. Our division was now called forward to clear up the situation to the west of the road. On the Sunday morning, 24 September, we moved off through Lommel, over the border into Holland and into Eindhoven, where we had to wait 24 hours in pouring rain due to the road being blocked further north. Next evening we were off again up the road through Son to St Gedenroede, where we stayed in position the next day and night, being machine-gunned occasionally by stray parties of Jerries who appeared from time to time, seeking a soft part of the road to ambush supply columns. We exercised our guns, for a change, by firing at a windmill which was alleged to contain an OP. I don't know whether it did or not, but I'm afraid we burned down the windmill. The following morning we moved on to Veghel, then turned west to Dinther, where we blocked the road from `s-Hertogenbosch, which contained a large number of Germans. Next morning another of my old friends, Harry Parry, was killed. Having arrived and dug in hastily in the dark, he decided at first light that it would be wise to have some more ammo handy, so he sent his chaps back to the half-track to fetch it whilst he stayed on watch by the gun. A stray mortar bomb landed by the gun pit, killing him instantly. His wife was expecting a baby that month. There were now only two of us who had been with the platoon since 1941 and less than half the platoon had been with the company in the desert. In fact that was the last casualty suffered by the platoon; we were lucky in the last six months of the war in escaping serious trouble. That was because we were nearly always advancing, with the anti-tank guns following the leading troops; it was when being attacked (as in the desert) that we were likely to suffer.

That afternoon we were relieved by the Queens and moved three miles north to Nistelrode and after a couple of days there, went forward two miles to the bigger village of Heesch, where we were to stay for almost three weeks. It was a fairly quiet time; the Germans had been pushed back far enough to make the supply line to Nijmegen safe and the division was holding a fourteen-mile line facing west, where Jerry was holding `s-Hertogenbosch, whilst plans were made for the next advance. The two armies were well apart and we took the opportunity to do a bit of maintenance and cleaning up, interrupted on only a couple of occasions. Once, a German battalion attacked the village of Geffen, just north of us, but were seen off by A Company. The church tower in Geffen had the best view of the countryside around and the Germans had been shelling it for days in an effort to knock it down, so in the end they attacked it (it was still standing when we left). Whilst this was going on, we were also shelled in Heesch, and I still have a letter from a young Dutchman, Leo, with whom we had made friends, saying, 'As they were shelling yesterday our quiet village, we find it necessary to go away from here. We took all the half-sleeping children and departed. The family could no more take any risks and of course I had to go with them. I am thinking it is a very pity that it almost will be impossible to continue our usual evening conversations. It were pleasant evenings and I was glad every time I had the opportunity to come to you. I must say I learned much from you. I'll take care that I don't forget the lot of words and expressions. I hope that I will been able to use this increased knowledge for the best purpose I could use it viz. the army itself ... Finally I will thank you for the pleasant time I could spend with you.'

The other occasion was when they put down a barrage on Vinkel, just to the southwest, but no attack developed. There was one amusing incident when the platoon commander went out on a recce patrol with a sergeant and one of the riflemen. Cautiously making their way forward in single file, the platoon commander came across a fallen telegraph wire across the path, about three feet above the ground. He carefully lifted it above his head with both hands and moved on; the sergeant did the same. But the rifleman bringing up the rear walked straight into the wire and made a terrible clatter. When they got back to the safety of Platoon HQ they asked him why he'd tripped over the wire and he replied, 'Well, I saw the officer put his hands up and walk forward, then the sergeant put his hands up and walked forward, so I put my hands up and walked forward and tripped over the bleeding wire'.

On 20 October we moved off on the next operation, clearing the ground up to the Maas. The Welsh Div. were to take 's-Hertogenbosch and the 15th (Scottish), Tilburg and we were to pass between them. We were hanging about in the area of Dinther and Middelrode for five days whilst the division was helping in the attack on 's-Hertogenbosch. Then over the next week we edged our way forward through Schijndel, south of Boxtel, and Helvoirt, Udenhout, Heikant (on the outskirts of Tilburg) and Dongen, near where our motor companies captured a fairly strong position, taking 120 prisoners, and finally to Klein Dongen. From here we relieved the Highland Div. in Raamsdonk and Raamsdonksveer, about 1,000 yards short of the Maas. The Germans were still south of the Maas at Geertruidenberg until they were pushed out by the Poles. We spent a fortnight here with a couple of breaks back at Company HQ at Klein Dongen. Shelling was quite heavy at times and I spent some evenings sitting on top of Raamsdonksveer Town Hall 'flashspotting'. We used to take a compass bearing on the flash, count how long before the bang and note the time. This information was passed back to the gunners and collated with other reports so that they could try and get a fix on where the batteries were located. We did the same when we saw V2 rockets going off. Whilst we were in this area we got our third gun back, with sufficient men to form a crew. The weather was getting colder and about this time we were issued with 'zoot suits', waterproof overalls lined with flannel which zipped up and had plenty of pockets. They were a very great benefit in the cold weather that was to come. Worn over battledress with a leather jerkin on top and, if necessary, a greatcoat as well, we were able to keep fairly warm.

October 1944

> *We are moving around pretty fast at the moment, as you can guess. It makes a bit of a change after being stuck in one spot for a time. We just missed catching a couple of Jerries the other day, the platoon commander and I were recce-ing positions and we strolled through a small belt of trees entirely ignorant of the fact that there were a couple of Jerries, one of them an officer, hiding in there with 'bazookas'. They gave themselves up to some of our chaps who went near there about five minutes later, but, as we said at the time, 'Fancy letting a couple of perfectly good wrist watches get away from us like that.'*

On 15 November we moved right across the front through Tilburg back into Belgium, through Turnhout and back through Geel and Mol to Lommel, Peer and Neeroeteren, west of Maeseyck. Here we had a fortnight's rest. We were billeted in private houses – our Platoon HQ was with the Nergeay family, mother and father (a photographer), son and daughter. We got on very well and corresponded for some time afterwards. Their only complaint was that the platoon commander didn't wash the bath round after he'd used it, whereas the 'other ranks' did! They didn't seem to mind us sleeping in their dining room. One letter we had from them later said 'Your friends of Neeroeteren will always keep the sweetest memory about their friends in the Rifle Brigade.' We soon got down to gun drill, weapon training and sorting out all our kit and cleaning it up, but the highlight for me was a 48-hour leave in Brussels. It was a five-hour journey by truck and we stayed in a school near the Parc du Cinqueantenaire, which had been taken over as a leave centre. Brussels was undamaged, the shop windows were all dressed for Christmas and it was fascinating just walking around seeing the sights or making our way by tram. These seemed to rattle around everywhere and we just jumped on, free to troops, and waited for somewhere familiar to come in sight before hopping off. The civilian restaurants were out of bounds but there was a sergeants' club where the food was quite good. I went to the pictures and saw *The Battle of Britain* (in French) and was forcibly reminded by a hissed 'Service, m'sieu' that in Belgium one is expected to tip the usherette. The two days went very quickly and we were off back to Neeroeteren, where we found that the company had already left. The Nergeays put us up for the night and I delivered some photographic plates he had asked me to get for him in Brussels.

Next morning we drove to rejoin the company at Born, in Holland once again, just beyond Sittard and right on the German border. Here the battalion was holding a couple of miles of front along the Vloed Beek, which was quite a fast-flowing stream about 30 feet wide. One company was in the village of Nieuwstadt and another at Holtum, a place we called the chateau because it had a dry moat around it and an internal courtyard with the buildings round the four sides. The third company was in reserve. We had one platoon in each of the positions, so we spent four days at Nieuwstadt, two days back at Born, four days at Holtum, another two days back at Born and so on. We left the guns in position each time rather than pulling them in and out of the gun pits every four days. At Nieuwstadt our guns were in back gardens, so we were able to live in the houses (the inhabitants had fled) except when on guard or stand-to, but at Holtum we were out in the open and had to sleep in slit trenches. This was no joke when the snow was thick and we had trouble stopping the half-tracks from freezing up; we were reluctant to start them up at night because Jerry could hear them and might pin-point our positions. They were the other side of the Vloed Beek, but were nearer to the river than us, which meant they could always get down to the river first at dusk and their patrols therefore tended to dominate no-man's-land. We pinched sheets, curtains, etc. from the houses to provide white camouflage for our guns and vehicles in the snow. I'm afraid the people must have found their houses in a bit of a mess when they got back to them.

As platoon sergeant I had to go back to Company HQ on most days for rations and mail and so on. I felt a bit exposed driving along the open road in full view but Jerry never opened up on us; he probably couldn't spare the ammunition on a small target. The roads were icy, which made the trip adventurous as it was. There was quite a lot of shelling when we first arrived, but the RHA had a 'ten for one' policy of retaliation and it soon quietened down to the odd salvo or occasional mortar bomb or burst of Spandau. The commander of C Company was unlucky enough to be killed by a leaflet shell which penetrated his cellar and landed in his lap. Most of the activity was at night, with patrolling by the motor companies. We were very thin on the ground, with a considerable gap between our posts at Nieuwstadt and Holtum, so we had to keep a sharp lookout when on guard (somehow all the bushes seem to start moving) and also try to keep warm without moving around and giving our positions away. Christmas Day was spent at Holtum. We were able to eat tinned turkey, but the drinking and merrymaking had to wait until we got back to Born two days later. Some Jerries were seen chasing chickens round a deserted farmhouse in no-man's land and as both sides used to visit it in search of eggs, we regarded this as an unfriendly act and fired a few bursts over their heads to discourage them. New Year's Day was spent in Nieuwstadt, so we didn't celebrate that either – probably just as well in view of the struggle I had getting the chaps to bed after a delayed Christmas binge. New Year's Day brought another spot of excitement. The Luftwaffe had massed all its strength for an attack on the RAF's airfields, over 250 planes being destroyed or damaged on the ground, and a number of them came roaring back over our heads at low level, giving me a chance to use my .5 Browning on its turret ring on the half-track, without hitting anything. We were amused to see that the Jerries opened up on the planes as well, they were so used to treating all aircraft as hostile. One night the Luftwaffe dropped their bombs on the German side of the Vloed Beek, perhaps in retaliation?

On 3 January we were relieved by the Devons and moved back a few miles to Geleen for a week's rest, billeted in houses. Our platoon had fifteen houses, two to a house. Ours contained five daughters between the ages of eighteen and twenty-four and the fact that I was the one who went on ahead to recce the billets was sheer coincidence. We were able to unload the trucks and get ourselves sorted out, and I was busy with the usual admin chores, but snowballing with the daughters was a popular pastime and there was a company dance. By now we had got our fourth gun back, so we were up to strength again. Manpower was still a problem and they had had to disband 50 Div. to provide reinforcements for other units. Two of their battalions, the Devons and Durhams, came to our 131 Brigade, where the three battalions of the Queens, much under strength, were amalgamated into one. This enabled them to produce sufficient people to bring our battalion up to strength again.

December 1944

They picked the names for home leave yesterday, and I expect to be home early in February. It has all been arranged in true RB fashion, whereby all the B Echelon wallahs, who landed in July, a month after us, are well to the fore in the first leave party. So when you read in the papers that the first batch of 'D-Day heroes' are home, take it with a couple of large sacks of salt! As an example, out of 28 men from the company going on leave in January, only one is from our platoon, although we actually form one-fifth of the total number to go. On the other hand, out of four men on the colour sergeant's truck in B Echelon, well back, three are in the first party!

Jerry seems to have come out of his shell at last, and to be having a final fling. On the whole, it should turn out a pretty good thing for us in the long run (except, of course, for the poor unfortunates who bore the brunt of the first attack). We've been waiting for a chance to catch him in the open for a long time, and provided the weather remains OK for flying, he is going to cop a packet. We have had a few Jerries over the last few nights but unfortunately one or two of them made a mistake and dropped their eggs on their own troops, much to our joy!

Home leave started while we were here and was the cause of much discontent. The press at home managed to give the impression that it was a case of first out, first back, so that the people who landed on D-Day would be in the first party, the D + 1 people next, and so on. But of course it did not work like that; only a limited number of men could be away from each unit at a time and a unit that arrived three months after D-Day would still be sending its quota with the first party. In our company they drew lots, and only one of our platoon got in the January list, although a fair share would have been six. However, three out of four of the colour sergeant's staff at B Echelon were in the first party, as was the company commander, with our platoon commander in the second, so they weren't complaining. As it would take about five months to work through the company, the chaps were a bit fed up. I was lucky because I got my leave in February.

After a week we went back to Nieuwstadt for four days, then returned to Geleen, to different billets. Only three daughters this time, but the Liebrechts were a very happy family and we had a lot of fun. The two sons were miners, as well as being champion milers, and took us along to the pithead baths for a shower. One of them was in the Resistance, having been in the army in 1940. I think it was the father at our previous billet who was the stationmaster, but he did not have much to do as no trains were running. We did promise the girls we would nip across the German border and get them a wireless set from a German house, but unfortunately did not get the opportunity until much later.

January 1945

It has been pretty cold lately, and the roads are like glass, but we are sitting pretty at the moment in the best billet we've ever had. They are a pretty large family, with four sons and three daughters at home – they are just about the cheeriest and most happy-go-lucky family I've ever seen. The two older sons have both been champion one-mile runners of Holland. One of them is a corporal in the Resistance Movement – he was in the army in 1940. The younger two are brimful of mischief, and my sides have been aching with laughter. I've laughed more since we've been here than in all the rest of the time we have been over here. They do nearly all of our cooking, and every time we try to get into the kitchen to wash up, we are forcibly ejected!

By now the platoon commander was on leave and I was in charge of the platoon. We were called to a conference to be told of operation Blackcock, which meant the division advancing north from our positions in Nieuwstadt and Holtum to clear the area up to the River Roer. 131 Brigade were to capture Susteren and Echt, then our brigade would go through to take St Joost, Montfort and St Odilienberg. It was only possible because of the hard frost, which enabled the tanks to operate over the low-lying and marshy ground with many ditches and canals. In the event, a thaw set in in the later stages, turning the ground into a quagmire and breaking up the one main road in our area.

The attack commenced on 17th January and we hung about at Born for three days waiting for 131 Brigade to complete their task. We eventually moved just after midnight on the 20th, by fits and starts, through Holtum, Susteren and Echt whilst I Company, helped by a troop of Crocodile Flamethrowers, were attempting to capture St Joost. It was found to be held by a battalion and not by a company and after sustaining considerable casualties they had to wait for help from the Durhams, who made an unsuccessful night attack, by which time we had moved to Schilberg where we were heavily shelled all night. Next day they managed to clear the village and gradually pushed on to Montfort, to which we moved at 1 am on the 24th. It was a sad sight because the RAF had given it a pasting as a prelude to the attack, many of the houses had been wrecked and when we arrived they were still digging bodies out of the ruins, mainly women and children. It was surprising that they seemed to bear us no malice for the disaster we had brought on them, especially as there were no Germans in the village at the time. We had little time to dwell on it as we took up positions on the far side of the village and were promptly shelled for the rest of the day, all that night and next morning. After that it quietened down a bit, although they were still shelling for the next few nights. After a week, on the 31st, the platoon went forward to St Odilienberg, but due to the difficult positions up there, with no cover for vehicles, I remained back with Company HQ. For the next five days I took the rations etc. up for them, and two other platoons, every day, using a Jeep instead of the half-track as the track was a sea of mud. On one occasion we got stuck on the way back and had to stop there all night until we could winch ourselves out in the morning.

By now my leave was due. I should have gone on 4 February, but it had twice been postponed due to bad weather (fog, I think, in the Channel) and I eventually left on the 6th to go back to B Echelon. My last job on the day I left was to help recover and bury the body of a

Canadian Typhoon pilot from the wreckage of his plane which had crashed into a sewer about a fortnight before – not a pleasant task. Next morning B Echelon transport took us to Niewstadt, where the divisional RASC picked us up and took us to Bourg Leopold, where we boarded the train at 6 pm, arriving at Calais at 6 am next morning. We spent the morning in the transit camp and sailed on the Princess Maud at 3.20 pm, finally arriving home at 8.15 in the evening. I spent the leave fairly quietly, enjoying the rest and a dry bed to sleep in. It was extended by a day because of more fog in the Channel, and the train left Victoria just before midnight on Saturday, 17 February, arriving at Dover at 2.30 am but then hanging around in Connaught Barracks until after midday. After we got to Calais we were hanging around again for a further seven hours before getting the train to Bourg Leopold, which we reached next morning, and transport then took us back to the company at Maeseyck.

The battalion had been resting at Maeseyck for about a week and it was to be another five weeks before we were called forward again – two weeks in Maeseyck where we were billeted in a convent, and the rest of the time in Someren, east of Eindhoven, where we were in a farmhouse. It was not a happy time; in the words of those days, we were browned off. The thrill of the quick dash across France and Belgium had long gone, and for months we had been roaming around in this land of rivers and canals, dykes and floods; it was cold and wet. The 'big one' was still to come – we had to get across the Rhine and into Germany, which no one believed would be easy. We were anticipating trouble from their equivalent of the Home Guard, which in fact did not materialise at all. More immediately we were back to drill parades, gun drill, maintenance, lectures and firing guns and small arms on the ranges, as well as inspections by the brigadier and by the colonel commandant. There were one or two games of soccer. The platoon could not have been too good as I see we lost 6 – 0 to Company HQ (the CSM was a very good footballer) and 12 – 0 to the machine gunners of 17 Platoon but we managed to draw 0 – 0 with 6 Platoon. Someren was a little better, as we were dispersed over a wider area and reverted to vehicle cooking which we always preferred.

Germany

❦

On 24 March the attack across the Rhine was launched at Wesel and Rees, preceded by an airborne landing; the sky was full of Dakotas and gliders as we prepared to move. We set off next day at midday, crossed the border into Germany north of Venlo and stopped for the night at Westerbroek, where we hung about all next day waiting for the bridge over the Rhine to be completed; in the end we had to wait another night. We spent the next day moving up to Xanten where we crossed the river on the Bailey bridge at 5.40 pm and got as far as Hamminkeln. The going was slow at first as the villages near the river had been turned into rubble by the bombing. Then we passed through the area where the 6th Airborne had landed, littered with gliders and discarded parachutes. Next morning we set off out of the bridgehead in our armoured regimental groups, the division's objective being Hamburg, 190 miles away. We got as far as Brünen, then it was stop and start as the tanks and motor companies cleared up pockets of resistance on the way. We eventually stopped for the night about four miles beyond Raesfeld. Some of the villages and woods were held by perhaps a company of Germans with a few guns which required a properly organised attack by the motor company to drive them out. At other times it was just an odd chap with a panzerfaust (bazooka) by the side of the road trying to knock out the leading tank or carrier at a few yards range. The civilian population largely disappeared from sight but many of the houses had white sheets hanging from the upstairs windows.

Next day it was evening before we moved on to Weseke where we dug in until the next evening (Good Friday), when we moved forward once again to a position between Sudlohn and Stadtlohn. After a night there we started off again the following afternoon but our half-track broke down with a blown gasket. It was a bit eerie being stuck all on our own in the middle of Germany but we were able to effect the repair without incident and pressed on to catch up with the company at Ahaus, only to find that our platoon had dropped off on the way to join A Company at Wullen. I went back but was unable to find them in the dark, so we did not rejoin until next morning. Once again the move did not come until the afternoon when we went back through Ahaus to take up positions north of Nieuborg; we changed position again twice the next day in response to real or imagined threats. As all the bridges over the Ems had been blown, there was a bit of a hold-up until the division got permission to use a bridge in the 11th Armoured Div. sector. 131 Brigade went across to Ibbenburen, in the Teutoburger Wald, but met the toughest resistance the division had come up against in Germany consisting of officer cadets and NCOs from a training school. Our brigade bypassed this by using the 11th Armoured Div. centre line, so next morning we moved off towards Burgsteinfurt, where our platoon commander went down with suspected diphtheria, leaving me in charge of the platoon for the last month of the war. He came back later, but as second-in-command of the company. Next day we went on through Emsdetten and Halen and over the Dortmund-Ems Canal, carrying on next day to Engter where we set up a road block and were fired on by both 20 mm and 88 mm guns. The following morning we moved on to Diepholz where we occupied the airfield, being prepared to take on any German planes that might try to land with our anti-tank guns!

Next morning we went off east through Rehden to Sulingen, where we were blocking the road to the south whilst a bridge was sought over the Weser, but they had all been blown. Next day we moved to Heiligerfelde and then to Syke, just south of Bremen. Here we dug in overnight, luckily, as we were attacked by an infantry battalion and some tanks, including a couple of Tigers, next morning. Fortunately, the Tigers did not come our way (one of them was knocked out by the divisional anti-tank regiment who had 17-pounders) but some of the shelling was too close to be funny. After they had been seen off we moved to take up a position with C Company at Barrien, and next morning tackled a party of Jerries who were trying to get at our tanks with panzerfausts – one was killed and we took the other five prisoner. It was now decided that an armoured division was not suitable to try to capture Bremen, so we had to stay in position for a couple of days until we were relieved by the Royal Norfolks of 3 Div. On 11 April we moved off at dusk to rejoin the company south of Syke and the following morning we moved southeast to the outskirts of Nienburg. There we lost our fourth gun again to provide reinforcements for the motor companies who were suffering a steady drain of casualties in their village and wood clearing activities. On the 15th we moved on again, over the Weser to Stockem, just short of Rethem on the Aller, where once again we bumped stray parties of Germans. We were off again next morning through Rethem and Fulde to Jarlingen to block the road there, and next day through Frielingen to Wiedingen, north of Soltau which we bypassed. Near here was the POW camp at Fallingbostel and amongst the 10,000 British and American prisoners who were released was Jock Callan, one of our sergeants who had been taken prisoner at Villers Bocage the previous June. We just happened to bump into him. He looked very thin but cheerful at being released and we were able to provide him with sufficient liquid refreshment to go on his way in a happy frame of mind.

The next day's move was across Lüneburger Heath to Weseloh and the day after to Tostedt and at last light to Sprotze. The following

At Fallingbostel, April 1945. Ken third from left

afternoon we got to Rade on the autobahn south of Hamburg where, for some reason, we had to lay a telephone cable to Company HQ instead of keeping the usual wireless watch (perhaps they wanted a full night's sleep at Company HQ). The cable kept getting broken by vehicles and we had to go out and repair it. As it was pouring with rain, which kept on all night, we got thoroughly wet. As we were still there next morning, we rapidly requisitioned a house, throwing the Germans out. Under the anti-fraternisation rules we were not allowed to be under the same roof as Germans, so it was a case of '*Sie müssen diese Haus verlassen in halbe Stunde*' ('You have to leave this house in half an hour'). We stayed there all day, moving on next morning through Moisberg to Buxtehude, almost on the Elbe west of Hamburg, where we moved into a naval barracks populated, until we arrived, almost entirely by German Wrens. I'm not sure where they were moved to, but they were buzzing about like bees from an upturned hive. Our only casualty was our RSM, who had his foot stamped on by one of the largest of them. Popular opinion was that they were no competition for the British variety. We expected to be here for one or two days but in fact remained for ten, although we moved out of the barracks into a house. Germany was starting to collapse and various negotiations for surrender got underway, the main objective of the Germans being to surrender to us rather than to the Russians. This culminated in the surrender of Hamburg on 3 May, and we went in to occupy Hamburg on the south bank of the Elbe. The company commander had a street map from which I was able to make a quick sketch of my area, which was centred on the '*Stadt Theater*'. However, when we got into the town, all we found were mounds of rubble which had been bulldozed aside in places in order to make roads. Here and there one could see puffs of smoke coming out, indicating that people were living somewhere underground. We wandered around looking for our area, occasionally bumping into one of our other platoons on a similar task and arguing about where we were. Eventually I just happened to spot one wall standing with the word '*Theater*' above the door, so decided we were in position, not that there was anything to do except drive round our area and gaze at the devastation.

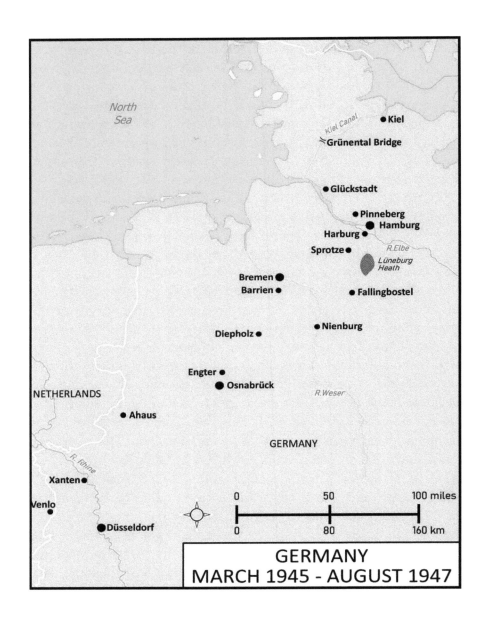

North
Sea

Kiel Canal

● Kiel

Grünental Bridge

● Glückstadt

● Pinneberg
● Hamburg

Harburg ●

Sprotze ●

R.Elbe

Lüneburg
Heath

Bremen ●

● Fallingbostel

Barrien ●

● Nienburg

Diepholz ●

Engter ●

● Osnabrück

R.Weser

NETHERLANDS

● Ahaus

GERMANY

R. Rhine

Xanten ●

0	50	100 miles
0	80	160 km

Venlo ●

● Düsseldorf

GERMANY
MARCH 1945 - AUGUST 1947

Hamburg, May 1945

The following afternoon the platoon commanders went to recce positions at Pinneberg, a few miles north of Hamburg. I found this somewhat scary. There were five or six officers and sergeants in a civilian car which someone had 'liberated', and we crossed the Elbe and drove through Hamburg up the road to Pinneberg passing swarms of fully-armed German troops at various camps on the way. Although negotiations were going on, there had been no formal surrender and there was nothing to stop any of these Jerries opening up on us. However there was no trouble and after spending a few somewhat nervous hours waiting at Pinneberg, the company turned up at 8 pm.

Three-quarters of an hour later a message came through: 'All German troops in northwest Germany and Denmark will surrender to 21ˢᵗ Army Group at 0800 hours tomorrow.' We got through that night and at eight next morning, 5 May, as far as we were concerned it was all over, although VE Day was not until the 8ᵗʰ.

Recce party – Harburg, May 1945

May 1945

We are still trying to get used to the idea that it's all over. One or two Jerries have come up to us with the weird idea that 'it's all over now, we can be friends again.' We soon sent them off with a flea in their ears ...

I've never seen a sight like Hamburg, it is literally 'flattened', just huge piles of rubble and bricks, with here and there smoke coming from a stove-pipe in an air raid shelter. Shelters are about the only places still habitable.

Where we are at the moment it's an amazing sight to see the Jerries pouring back along the road – driving themselves in trucks, or in horses and carts, or just on foot. We've had to give up taking them in now – we just disarm them and tell them to hop it; it is impossible to look after them and feed them all.

Somehow it was something we could not comprehend. They may have been dancing in the streets of London but with us it was greeted almost in silence. Indeed, on VE Day I was so struck by how miserable everybody looked that I got my camera out and took a photo. Not that we were not relieved. It had been a very long road and many had not

"Just another day" – Pinneberg, VE Day 1945

reached the end. The battalion had lost about 150 killed since June, and I would guess at least twice as many as that were wounded, so we must have lost two-thirds of our strength in all. Some of us had not expected to come through unscathed either, but in the anti-tank company we had a relatively cushy time in Europe. Apart from the normal risks from shelling, mortaring, mines etc., one is most at risk on an anti-tank gun when the enemy attacks, and that was rare in this campaign. It has been said with some truth that the anti-tank gunner was either bored to tears or qualified for a posthumous VC. The motor companies, on the other hand, were always going forward clearing villages and woods and therefore exposed to fire from a hidden enemy. Danger was always present and we rarely talked about 'after the war', except in joking terms. The army had been preparing for this; they set up the Army Bureau of Current Affairs which issued pamphlets and organised lectures on what would or should happen in Britain after the war but this was not for us and we were always too busy anyway. So when it finally ended we were totally unprepared mentally, except for the standing joke that the initials of our official postal address – British Liberation Army – also stood for Burma Looms Ahead. But for the moment we were kept busy where we were, although I had time to think also of all my old school friends who had not made it – about twenty from my year (about one in five) and many others whom I had also known. A lot of them had been in the RAF or Fleet Air Arm.

Our divisional commander at the end of the war, Major General Verney, wrote 'They were great battalions, those battalions of the Queens Royal Regiment, and they had a record of continuous front-line service that could probably not be equalled by any other infantry of the Eighth Armies or Second Armies, save their friends and colleagues of the 7th Armoured, the 1st Battalion, The Rifle Brigade'.[5]

---

[5] Major-General G. L. Verney, D.S.O., N.V.O., in foreword to Wingfield R. M., *The Only Way Out*.

Army of Occupation

We spent the next two days waiting at Pinneberg, and at midday on the 7th moved off through Elmshorn and Itzehoe and up to the Kiel Canal where we mounted guard on a bridge at Grünental. We were hoping to go in to liberate Denmark but unfortunately this was not to be. The immediate problem for the army was to cope with the hundreds of thousands of German soldiers, sailors and airmen who were anxious to surrender to us rather than to the Russians. Some were trying to 'demob' themselves and make their own way home, together with all the displaced persons of many nationalities – French, Belgian, Dutch, Polish, Czech, Lithuanian, Latvian, Estonian, Russian, etc. They had been on forced labour in Germany and were now trying to make their way home or, if they lived in Russian-occupied countries, trying not to be sent home. When one added all the German civilians who had moved westwards to avoid the Russians, it sometimes seemed as if the whole of Europe was on the move. Our first orders were to allow the German troops to cross the bridge from north to south, but to turn back any trying to move north towards Denmark. These orders were quickly reversed and they were allowed to go north but not south. The object was to create an area – Peninsula C – between the Danish frontier and the Kiel Canal in which the Germans could be concentrated and dealt with at leisure, looking for any war criminals and arranging to send home first those needed for urgent reconstruction work.

However, an unexpected problem soon cropped up. I was called out to the bridge, where the sergeant in charge of the guard was a long-service regular who was known as 'Sir Jasper' because of his resemblance to the wicked squire of the old melodramas. He pointed out a convoy of ships coming down the canal, an escort vessel followed by half a dozen landing craft packed to the gunwales with

German sailors. We knew what to do with traffic on the road but had no orders about the canal, so I hastily got on the air to Company HQ who said, 'Wait one, we'll ask Battalion.' The ships were getting nearer and nearer when eventually the reply came back, 'Stop them and find out what they are doing.' This made me scratch my head because our 6-pounders could not be depressed sufficiently to fire into the canal and we couldn't go blazing away into the countryside now the war was over. Anyway, the gun on the escort vessel was bigger than ours. So I fired a burst of Sten across their bows and to my relief they stopped engines. I sent the sergeant down the umpteen steps to the waterside and he returned with the German naval officer in charge, who said that under the orders of the Senior British Naval Officer at Kiel, the men were being moved down to Brunsbuttel as there was no accommodation for them at Kiel. In due course word came back from Brigade via Battalion and Company to let them pass. He accompanied the officer back down the steps and there was a fierce altercation after he went on board and the convoy moved on. When he returned I found that he had 'liberated' the officer's wrist watch. I called him all the names under the sun and half expected our own navy to send a warship up to recover it if the officer complained, but I never heard any more.

P.O.W. barge - Grünental Bridge, May 1945

Guard detail – Grünental Bridge, May 1945

May 1945

I am sorry I haven't written before but we have been kept pretty busy lately. We are taking care of about 100,000 Jerries till they get themselves demobbed. At the same time we are gradually getting ready to revert to a peacetime basis – bags of spit and polish, and all the rest of it.

The mail has been held up a bit by all the V E Day celebrations in England.

We spent two or three weeks in various villages in the area, patrolling and locating arms dumps and guarding the 'Stop line' at Albersdorf to prevent any unauthorised exits. We then spent a month at Gokels, south of the canal, where we got down to drill, vehicle, gun and equipment maintenance, current affairs lectures and colonel's inspection. We had a couple of inter-platoon football matches and the band, which had come out from England, gave a concert which the sergeants supplemented with a few sketches. The battalion had only two sets of football boots, so each company could use them only once a week, and we had no cricket bats or stumps. Later on we got much more equipment – I had more sports kit in my store than military equipment.

Despite the strict non-fraternisation policy with the Germans in force at this time, keeping troops and girls apart was virtually impossible. I could understand the troops but was surprised by the attitude of the girls, whom I would have thought would still have been full of 'hate'. However, there were few young German men about; they had suffered enormous casualties and most of the survivors were still in prison camps, certainly the younger ones. So the girls had been deprived of male company whilst from the troops they would get cigarettes, which rapidly became the main black market currency, and could purchase almost anything. What always puzzled me was that after passing from hand to hand in endless transactions, someone must eventually have paid a high price to smoke the things, if they were still intact. They might also get chocolate and occasional tins of food – many of them seemed to be living mainly on potatoes at that time. Provided the troops were discreet, one turned a blind eye to this 'fratting', but sometimes they went a bit too far. On one occasion I returned to our platoon billet from Company HQ and immediately caught a whiff of scent, noticed that one of the chaps was missing and that the door of his room was locked. My order to open the door meeting no response, I burst it open in time to see the girl disappearing out of the open window clutching half her clothes. I felt that doing it under my nose was just too much. Later, dances were organised with girls from a DP (displaced persons) camp nearby, but some of the lads used to appear with girls who could not speak Polish or any other language except German. After a couple of months the order was rescinded.

On 23 June we moved to Glückstadt, on the north bank of the Elbe halfway between Hamburg and the sea, which was to be the battalion's home for the next year. At first we were in billets in the town (our platoon was in the Hotel Bahnhof in town) but in December we moved into a nearby naval barracks. The first ten days we spent settling in, during which I got caught for the ceremonial battalion quarter guard, then for ten days I was acting CSM whilst the CSM was busy organising and drilling the 90 men we needed to provide a guard at Corps HQ 70 miles away. Then I had ten days leave; truck to Itzehoe then Hamburg, then a 3 am train to Celle, Hannover, Minden (alight for dinner), Osnabruck,

Munster, Rees, Gennep (alight for tea), Schijndel, Tilburg, Mechelen, Schaerbeek and St Omer to Calais where we arrived at 6.30 am the following morning, to find that sailing was delayed for 24 hours. We finally left the following afternoon and I got home on Sunday evening having left Glückstadt on Thursday afternoon.

I got back on the afternoon of 6 August. There was a lot of reorganisation going on, people being moved around, going on courses, etc. There were also plenty of duties to do including battalion quarter guard, company guard, MT picquet, harbour ferry guard, a brewery guard and, from time to time, curfew patrol and patrols of the surrounding countryside. It was difficult to find the people for all these activities, what with people on leave and on courses (there were quite a lot of educational courses to help people prepare for 'civvy' life). There were also quite a lot of inter-unit transfers. Being a regular battalion which would remain in being, many of the younger soldiers with longer to serve were transferred to us, whilst some of our older chaps were transferred to our 8th Battalion which, being a Territorial Battalion, was stood down in April 1946. I was myself in a state of uncertainty. An attempt at a correspondence course in higher mathematics convinced me that there was no point in trying to return to my previous occupation and the study that it would involve, and one or two other ideas came to nothing. I took the coward's way out and volunteered to stay on for an extra year to give myself time to sort something out. In the end this worked out very well. As a result I was promoted to colour sergeant (company quartermaster sergeant), and in consequence spent most of the rest of my time in my office rather than on the square. It was a very good life, with work confined mainly to the mornings and the afternoons devoted to sport.

November 1945

So far there have been two cancellations of leave, which means I'm now due home on Dec. 2nd.

Demob is very much in the air at the moment, as all sergeants and over in the battalion are likely to be deferred, as there is an acute shortage of NCOs.

Talking of sergeants, they made me up to Colour-bloke the other day, with effect from 25 September, so I've been feverishly sewing crowns on top of my stripes all over the place. At the moment we're engaged in dishing out winter woollies.

At one time we expected to go to Berlin, as the division was sent there for the Victory Parade at the time of the Potsdam Conference with Churchill taking the salute, but as usual we were left behind. The troops were somewhat put out to see the British press full of photographs of the 'Desert Rats', when in fact they were the Devons and the nearest they had ever got to the desert was Malta, having only joined the division in the last months of the war. There was a similar feeling a year later, when the Victory March took place in London and the regiment was represented by recruits from the depot.

I did manage to get to Berlin, however, when playing rugger for the division against the British Troops in Berlin. We travelled in a hired German coach but they had been unable to get the appropriate pass for the driver, a wizened old man whom they hastily fitted out with an army greatcoat and a beret rammed on his head. Luckily the Russians did not inspect us too closely at any of the checkpoints. Berlin of course was still in ruins but we were able to have a look around. We found the Russian sector (and also the Russian Zone of Germany) quite eerie. Everything and everyone seemed so quiet and the Russian troops always looked so sullen and unsmiling compared with our own, who always had a laugh and a joke. Back in Glückstadt, apart from sport we found other amusements. Because cigarettes were in such great demand even dog-ends were valuable and we would be followed along the street by children or even men, waiting to grab the cigarette ends when we threw them away. The Company Sergeants' Mess at Glückstadt was on the ground floor, with a window opening onto the pavement. Occasionally we used to tie a dog-end on the end of a piece of cotton and drop it onto the pavement outside the window. As soon as anyone stooped to pick it up, we hauled in the cotton.

In December my turn for leave came round again, so I was home for Christmas for the first time since 1939. I was also lucky as the company was putting on a Panto, 'Ali Baba and the Forty Colour Sergeants', and I was cast as the wicked colour sergeant, and I was able to dodge this. My journey home was much simpler this time, but there was of course a twelve-hour wait before boarding the *Empire Rapier* which sailed from Cuxhaven the next morning on the 28-hour voyage to Hull. I left home at 5 pm on Boxing Day and got back to Glückstadt 48 hours later. I found the whole of the battalion had now moved into the barracks, which made things very much more regimental, especially as they brought some buglers over to blow us out of bed in the mornings and summon all and sundry with their calls. The RSM was able to have his beloved drill parades, the whole battalion ate together and we had a battalion Sergeants' Mess, presided over by the RSM.

The snow was very heavy for the first few months of 1946 which put paid to rugger for a bit. I spent my working time mainly in the office dealing with paperwork and checking weapons, equipment, clothing, stores, etc. I was still struggling with algebra and trigonometry but was also made Sergeants' Mess Treasurer, so had a chance to start some

Ken at his desk – Osnabruck, 1947

Official portrait – Osnabruck,

practical bookkeeping. In the months ahead I also had to come to the aid of my successors with their figure-work, as well as with the Officers' Mess and PRI (Welfare Funds) accounts.

In July 1946 we moved to Winkelshausen Barracks, Osnabruck, and things gradually returned to a peacetime regimental routine. The band came out from England, as did all the Mess silver – the Sergeants' Mess looked very smart when all the trophies were on display. We also had a number of senior NCOs who had been taken prisoner with the battalion at Calais and had signed on

again. This tended to split the Mess into two camps. One day, one of the 'ex-Kriegies' (POWs) thought we were reminiscing about the desert a bit too much, so he tipped all the sand from a fire-bucket on to the floor and said 'Now perhaps you'll be happy.' Next time we caught a few of them chatting at the bar about their prison camp a couple of us nipped down and brought up a coil of Dannert wire with which we enclosed them to make them feel at home. Their wives also came out and married quarters were established. We soon realised that Mrs Sergeant Major A regarded herself as senior to Mrs Sergeant B and it was very amusing to see on dance nights in the Mess the frosty looks they gave to some of the unmarried sergeants who brought in German girlfriends (by then 'fratting' was permitted).

During the evening of 25 August (regimental birthday) we came across a party of matelots wandering around the town in search of amusement. They proved to be the crew of an ML (motor launch) patrolling the Elbe. They were trying to find somewhere where they could be together and not separated according to rank, so we invited them into our Company Sergeants' Mess and had a very convivial evening which culminated in our helping them wheel the cox'n back to the ship in a wheelbarrow. To my horror they just upended the wheelbarrow and tipped him on to the deck – the tide had ebbed and there was a drop of seven or eight feet but he came to no harm. In return they invited us for a trip on the river, so the next afternoon (Sunday) we spent cruising down the Elbe. We spotted a trawler coming upstream and altered course to intercept. The skipper yelled '*Haben Sie Fisch?*' and on getting a '*Ja*' in reply we went alongside and a tin of cigarettes went one way and a basket of fish the other, which gave us a change of diet next day.

The barracks were much more comfortable by now – a lot more furniture had been provided and there were gangs of Germans to do maintenance work and other chores around the barracks. Those in the Sergeants' Mess were in the charge of a chap called Tex – because he had been a POW in the USA (from a U-boat) and spoke English with an American accent. Watching the way they worked (and the way he kept them at it) I was not surprised to see how rapidly Germany recovered from the devastated state it was in at the end of the war.

My last leave came on 2 February. I left the barracks at 9 am and got home via the Hook and Harwich at midday next day, in time to meet power cuts of two to three hours twice a day (we had the same thing in Osnabruck). While I was at home I went up to the city for an interview with Colonel Wilson of Albert Goodman & Co. to discuss the possibility of their taking me on as an articled clerk. This was provisionally agreed, subject to fixing the details after I was demobbed. I left home at midday on 22 February and got back to Osnabruck, via Harwich and the Hook (on the *Manxman*) the following evening, for my last few weeks in the army.

I managed three or four games of rugger and also some hockey and spent most of the time doing accounts. These had to be prepared monthly and by now I was not only doing those of the Sergeants' Mess and B Company but also helping most of the other companies as well as the Officers' Mess and PRI with theirs. I began to feel I was quite an accountant already, especially as I had been swotting up bookkeeping in the evenings.

By now my time in the army was coming to an end. Life was very pleasant, there was as much sport as ever, cricket, tennis and swimming having been added to the list, and also plenty of congenial company, but I had to get started on a career.

I handed over my duties on 14 April and was given a farewell party in the Mess on the 15th. With a considerable amount of sadness I finally left the battalion the following morning, but I only got as far as the transit camp at Munster – just over an hour away – and spent the rest of the day and night there, feeling somewhat lonely after leaving all my friends. The next morning I came back through Osnabruck in the train, then on to Hamburg where we changed trains. We continued to Cuxhaven where we boarded the *Empire Halberd* and sailed late that night. We arrived in Hull at ten the following night but remained on board until the morning. We then disembarked and went by train to York where we spent four hours going through the demobilisation process at Fulford barracks.

Apart from the paperwork it was a matter of collecting civilian clothing (I preferred a sports coat and flannels to the suit on offer), raincoat, hat, shoes and shirt, etc. I also received a ration book, clothing coupons and identity card. I had release leave of 117 days in all and I was still on the strength until 14 August 1947. The formalities completed, I caught the train to London and got home just after midnight with seven years, seven months and twenty-four days in uniform to look back on. For nearly six years and four months of this my address had been B Company, 1st Bn, The Rifle Brigade. It was a long time before I really felt myself to be a civilian again.

The
Post-War
Years

꧁꧂

*A Synopsis of of Ken's Life after
Demobilisation*

Hawker Siddeley Group
and Family Life

❦

After the war Ken spent a couple of weeks at home sorting his things out and buying clothes with his newly issued clothing coupons. He joined an accountancy firm called Albert Goodman & Co. as an articled clerk and started work on 5 May 1947. Their office was in the City of London, on the corner of Old Broad Street and London Wall. The job involved visiting various companies including a solicitor's office near the Strand in London, a baker in Winchmore Hill and the Officers' Mess at AA Command HQ at Bushey.

After he started work Ken hastened to get all his articles signed and accepted by the Institute of Chartered Accountants. He sat his final in May 1950. The duration of articles was reduced to three years due to his war service but still required many hours of hard work. This did not leave a lot of time for other activities but he did find time for rugger in the winter months. It took quite a time for Ken to get used to being a civilian again. Conversation could be difficult – in the army half of their language was unprintable and the other half was a mixture of Arabic, Hindustani, Maltese, Italian and German. At first he found it wise to count to ten before opening his mouth while he made a rapid mental check of what he was about to say.

In his spare time Ken played rugger for the Old Tiffinians, with the occasional walk on a Sunday with Old Tiffinians walking section. He missed the community feeling and good humour that is generated when a crowd of people are living together and which was inevitably absent in civilian life, where people dispersed to their homes every day. He enjoyed the rugger season when he could get together with some kindred spirits, all being ex-serviceman. At least 120 Old Boys were known to have been killed during the war and Ken remembered that about twenty of them were from his year at school.

One morning on the train up to London Ken bumped into a club member who said 'Daphne would like a word with you.' Daphne was the sister of another member of the rugger club and was secretary to one of the bigwigs at Hawker Siddeley Group. Somewhat mystified, Ken rang her up and was told that they had a vacancy which might be of interest to him. Ken felt he could not accept because he was committed to work for another year with his present firm. He felt this was a shame because an aircraft company would have been just as attractive to him as a shipping company, which had always been his preferred career choice as a teenager. However, a week later Daphne called again and asked if Ken would like to go and see her boss. Ken thought there was no harm in going for an interview – they might bear him in mind for later on. He had an interview with JF Robertson at the head office in St James' Square. He said, 'Go and discuss it with your principal – surely he wouldn't stand in your way?' Ken agreed to do so and the next morning received the result of his final exam, with the news that he had passed (420 passed out of the 994 who sat the exam). His principal told him that if it was a job he wanted he did not want to stand in his way, but he would have to work two months' notice. They eventually compromised at six weeks as Hawker Siddeley wanted him to start work on their annual accounts. He started work with Hawker Siddeley on Monday, 18 September 1949.

Hawker Siddeley Group was at this time engaged almost entirely in the aircraft industry. On his first morning at head office Ken reported to JF Robertson, the Group Treasurer. The Company Chairman was Thomas Sopwith. To Ken's surprise, the first job he was given was the Sopwith investment register. As Mr Sopwith (later Sir Thomas Sopwith) was a millionaire twice over, there was quite a lot involved. He owned estates at Compton Manor, Arkengarthdale (for the grouse), on the Isle of Harris (for the salmon and deer) and also a property in South Africa which he visited every year. His tax return was a major undertaking and at least once a year Ken and his colleagues had to prepare a statement of his assets.

Ken felt that there was also important work to be done on the company accounts, as the Group was expanding rapidly, but continued the Sopwith work for a further nineteen years until Young Tommy (Sir Thomas's son) arranged for his own accountant to take it all over. Ken and his colleagues' main task on the financial side was to prepare the annual accounts. Apart from looking after the Sopwith family affairs, they used to prepare calculations of the government profit formula for all the companies, which they had to agree with the accountants from the ministry. The tax liabilities for each of the companies also had to be worked out in conjunction with the auditors and agreed with the Inland Revenue. Ken was heavily involved in settling the Group's excess profits tax liabilities for the war years from 1937 to 1946.

In the meantime, at home Ken had taken some driving lessons. He had driven an assortment of vehicles in the army, but the Highway Code did not operate out there. He passed his test and bought a second-hand Austin A40 Devon from Hawksley, a Hawker Siddeley Group company, in 1953 for £250. They hadn't had a car in the family before and his mother used to enjoy being taken out for drives into the country on Sundays. The other exciting purchase for the family was a television set. They bought one in January 1953 in good time for the Queen's coronation later in the year.

This was the pattern for the next five years, during which Ken absorbed the atmosphere of the office, gained experience and with it, confidence. Apart from visits to companies at the end of the year, there were also visits to discuss other matters that arose, particularly to Gloucester to visit Hawksley, whose factory had come to the end of the pre-fab production and was being switched to the production of aero-engines.

Ken enjoyed a few walking holidays in the Pyrenees with friends and in 1953 he went to Austria on his own, booked through Inghams. He took the ferry from Dover to Ostend then a train via Munich to Innsbruck. Ken found it was a strange sensation being in Germany in civvies and not part of the army of occupation. He didn't have the same feeling in Austria. Ken's rugby career came to an abrupt conclusion in January 1955. They were playing against Barclays Bank near Hangar Lane, Ealing. Ken was kicking at a loose ball when someone must have kicked him on the right shin and, as was later found, broken his tib and fib. An ambulance took him to the Central Middlesex Hospital.

Ken had been dealing with the Sopwith family accounts for some time when, in November 1955, when going over the farm accounts, he was invited to lunch with Sir Thomas and Lady Sopwith. It was a very pleasant occasion although the conversation was not always easy to follow – references to Dickie and Charles coming to dinner turned out to be Lord Mountbatten and Prince Charles! Ken was made deputy group accountant in January 1956. Later that year he became involved for the first time with the affairs of AV Roe Canada (later to become Hawker Siddeley Canada). This involvement would require a great many business trips to Canada in the coming years. Also, in 1956, Ken was given a company car, an Armstrong Siddeley Sapphire 236. It had manumatic gears, which never caught on.

Ken at his desk – Hawker Siddeley, 1957 (Company Photo)

1957 proved to be a busy year. Ken used to see his future wife, Kathie, socially as her friend Brenda also worked for Hawker Siddeley. Kathie had previously worked for Hawksley in Brockworth. In the spring of 1957 they got together regularly, culminating in their getting engaged while sitting by the Silent Pool near Shere in Surrey on 22 June. They decided to get married in September and Kathie would start hunting for a flat which they could move into when they were married.

Meanwhile, Ken was very busy in the office. The future of the aircraft industry was in some doubt. Aircraft were becoming much more expensive to develop and fewer prototypes and production aircraft were being ordered. Hawker Siddeley Group was going to have to diversify into other sectors of engineering.

Ken and Kathie get married – September 1957

Kathie moved into a flat which she had found in Wimbledon. She and Ken were married on 14 September 1957 at St Margaret's Church in Putney. They spent their honeymoon in Austria before settling down to married life. The following spring they moved to a house in Carshalton Beeches, south of London, from where Ken was able to commute by train to his office in St James Square. A daughter, Ann, was born in 1959 and Christine followed in 1960.

As part of an internal reorganisation at Hawker Siddeley, Ken was appointed to the board of the holding company for the smaller operations of the Group. At the end of 1964 the government appointed a committee to look into the future of the aircraft industry and Ken was given the task of preparing the Group's submission. This required a great deal of work in collecting a lot of information from Group companies. Ken's title at Hawker Siddeley became Head of Group Planning, which he didn't really like very much. He did, however, enjoy most of his work which mainly involved delving into problems and exploring possibilities. He preferred to work on his own doing this, rather than 'sitting back and organising other people'.

The family moved from Carshalton Beeches to a house with a large garden in Sutton, Surrey in 1969. His wife Kathie sadly died of cancer in 1979. Ken remained working at Hawker Siddeley while his daughters were at school in Sutton. By 1983, both daughters had left home. Over the years the job had involved numerous trips abroad, mainly to Canada but also on occasions to the USA and to South Africa. Ken had enjoyed the travel but it was now becoming more of a chore. He decided that he was 'happy to settle down and be able to please myself instead of being continuously on the go.' Ken retired from Hawker Siddeley in August 1983 after 33 years spent working for the company. In his retirement he enjoyed many happy hours tending his garden, reading his extensive collection of military books and writing his memoirs. He also loved regular get-togethers with his daughters and their families.

Old age eventually made looking after the large house and garden an increasingly difficult task and Ken moved into a flat in sheltered accommodation in Ashford, Middlesex in 2005, close to where his

Ken with daughters Ann and Christine – 2010

younger daughter, Christine, lived. He settled well into his new home, continuing to enjoy a quiet and relatively independent life, despite living with dementia for his final few years. Ken died on 21 June 2013 at the age of 91, after leading a very full and happy life.

Glossary

❦

AA	Anti-Aircraft (as in 'AA gun')
B Echelon	The reserve and support elements of the battalion to the rear of the battlefield
Bir	Well (used in place names like Bir Gibni)
Bull	Polishing of kit, especially boots
Bully Beef	Tinned salt-cured beef
CLY	County of London Yeomanry
CCS	Casualty Clearing Station
CSM	Company Sergeant Major
Defiladed	Shielded from potential enemy fire by an obstacle or natural feature
ENSA	Entertainments National Service Association
Jebel	(Also Djebel) Arabic name meaning hill or range of hills
LCT	Landing Craft Tanks
LST	Landing Ship Tanks
Maquis	French Resistance group(s)
MO	Medical Orderly
Nebelwerfer	A German 6-barrelled mortar
OCTU	Officer Cadets Training Unit
OP	Observation Post
QM	Quartermaster – the officer responsible for supply
Portee	Vehicle for transporting anti-tank gun or other artillery piece
RASC	Royal Army Service Corps
RHA	Royal Horse Artillery
RSM	Regimental Sergeant Major
Sidi	Tomb of Holy Man (used in place names like Sidi Barrani)
Topee	Lightweight cloth-covered sun helmet also known as a pith helmet
Trigh	Long distance desert track
Very Light	Bright flare fired to illuminate an area
Wadi	Valley, ravine or channel that is dry except in the rainy season

Lightning Source UK Ltd.
Milton Keynes UK
UKHW050024010521
382916UK00007B/110